1951

THE GREAT BOOKS:

A CHRISTIAN APPRAISAL

VOLUME II

THE
GREAT BOOKS

A CHRISTIAN APPRAISAL

*A Symposium on the Second Year's Program
of the Great Books Foundation*

Edited by
Harold C. Gardiner, S.J.
Literary Editor of "America"

II

THE DEVIN-ADAIR COMPANY

NEW YORK

Printed in the United States of America

Foreword

THIS IS Volume II of the four-volume series *The Great Books: A Christian Appraisal.* It follows the scheme and the purpose of the first volume, namely, to evaluate by the standards of Christian thinking the books which are selected for study by the Great Books Foundation. As Volume I considered the first year's books in the Foundation's four-year course, so Volume II takes in order those used in the second year. The substantial success which Volume I attained, and the large measure of appreciation which was accorded it have greatly encouraged editor, contributors and publisher in the preparation of this second, larger volume.

Introduction

IN PRESENTING this second volume of *The Great Books: A Christian Appraisal* to the public which has accorded so warm a welcome to the first volume in the series, it strikes me that perhaps a few words are necessary once again to indicate the essential purpose of these studies.

The motive-idea behind the Great Books discussions is that the free interplay, the democratic give and take of conversation between the discussion leaders and the discussants, and among the discussants themselves, is the best way in which to arrive at some estimate of the greatness of the books chosen for study. With this general idea neither I nor any of the contributors to this series, I believe, have any serious quarrel. The Great Books discussions appeal, naturally, to adults—in fact, the very nature of the project makes it an excellent and promising tool for widespread adult education. But adults, whether they practice well or poorly the Gospel admonition to "become as little children," do not much relish, I suppose, becoming so like little children as to welcome a return to the little red schoolhouse, to slates, report cards and, it may be, to dunce caps.

In other words, we do not much like to be lectured to. And so, the Great Books Foundation rather wisely suggests that the discussion circles be not stuffily solidified into classrooms. There *is* a type of discussion which can plumb into the heart of the Great Books, and come away with clear, solid and useful knowledge of just what is the contribution the books have made to the sum total of human wisdom and perhaps even of human happiness.

But frankly, things do not too often work out that way. First of all, such fruitful discussion demands and very frequently does not get a most excellent discussion leader. Our ideal leader would be a man who knows the particular Great Book thoroughly, and all the other works of the author as well, for it is frequently only through a complete knowledge of a man's thought that one can appreciate and gauge nicely his particularized thought in *this* book. (This, I believe, is a truth well brought out in Professor' Mercier's analysis in this volume of Rousseau's two discourses.)

Our ideal discussion leader would have much more than knowledge, too. He would be graced with exquisite tact, with keen and gentle humor. He would have dialectical agility, in order to keep (if I may mix my metaphors horribly) the ball of discussion rolling and the topic on the beam. He would need—well, why go on? I think it is obvious, both *a priori* and to all who have attended such discussions, that the ideal leader would be a paragon.

Now, since such paragons are not come upon in many a day's journey, we offer you here something, we feel, that may somewhat fill in for the paucity of paragons. These essays are designed to get right at the heart of the Great Books they treat. Having read these essays, you will, we hope, be able to start your discussions with the real point at issue in each book. You are supplied with, so to speak, the topic sentence of the book—from there it will be easier and more fruitful to discover precisely wherein the greatness lies.

I know that some Great Book enthusiasts do not like this approach. They feel that it approximates what they try so hard to avoid, namely, intellectual spoon-feeding. Well, to them I can only say that those who have used the first volume in this series have declared that, if they were subjected to some spoon-feeding, what they were fed must have been full of intellectual vitamins, because the discussions meant very much more for them and they were able to contribute their share and more toward stimulating their fellow discussants.

As was necessary in introducing the first volume, I must remark here, too, that Catholic participants in the Great Books courses must recall to their minds that some books in the series are on the *Index of Forbidden Books*. This second volume contains one—Hobbes's *Leviathan*. Pascal's *Pensées* is not on the *Index*, unless it is the edition that contains the notes by Voltaire. Some permission (whether general or particular will depend on local circumstances and regulations) has to be obtained before these books on the *Index* can be read in their entirety for the purpose of later discussion. And, once again, may I ask non-Catholics who may happen to use this volume not to take this necessary caution that I must issue, as an occasion for hasty thoughts or statements to the effect that the *Index* is an unwarranted tampering with free intellectual inquiry. The very fact that many Catholics are taking part in the Great Books discussions is evidence to the contrary.

At any rate, here is Volume II of *The Great Books: A Christian Appraisal.* May it encourage the type of free intellectual inquiry that will strengthen both our democratic way of life and our fidelity to our Christian heritage. This double fruit is no strange fruit; it is rather the most natural in the world, for the two values stand shoulder to shoulder and march hand in hand.

HAROLD C. GARDINER

Contents

Foreword . . . . **v**

Introduction . . . . . Harold C. Gardiner   **vii**

HOMER: *The Odyssey* . . . Edwin A. Quain   **1**

HERODOTUS: *History, Books I and II*
                    Rudolph Arbesmann   **8**

AESCHYLUS: *House of Atreus (Agamemnon, The Choephori, The Eumenides)*
                    Rudolph Arbesmann   **17**

SOPHOCLES: *Oedipus Rex, Antigone*
                    Rudolph Arbesmann   **25**

ARISTOTLE: *The Poetics* . . Francis X. Connolly   **33**

PLATO: *Meno* . . . . . Balduin V. Schwarz   **43**

ARISTOTLE: *Ethics, Books II, IV and VI*
                Dietrich von Hildebrand   **51**

LUCRETIUS: *On the Nature of Things, Books I-IV*
                    Edwin A. Quain   **58**

MARCUS AURELIUS: *Meditations*
                    Rudolph Arbesmann   **66**

HOBBES: *Leviathan* . . . Waldemar Gurian   **74**

MILTON: *Areopagitica* . . . Victor M. Hamm   **81**

SWIFT: *Gulliver's Travels* . . . Riley Hughes   **88**

PASCAL: *Pensées* . . . . Jean Paul Misrahi   **98**

ROUSSEAU: *A Discourse on Political Economy, On the Origin of Inequality* . Louis J. A. Mercier 107

KANT: *Fundamental Principles of the Metaphysics of Morals* . . . . Gustave Weigel 122

NIETZSCHE: *Beyond Good and Evil*
                                    Charles Denecke 131

MILL: *Representative Government*
                                    Pacifico A. Ortiz 138

TAWNEY: *Religion and the Rise of Capitalism*
                                    Goetz A. Briefs 148

Notes on the Contributors 157

THE GREAT BOOKS:

A CHRISTIAN APPRAISAL

VOLUME II

Homer: The Odyssey

IN THE WORKS of Homer we find the beginning of the literary tradition of Western civilization. His shadowy figure (we know not a single detail of his life) loomed large in the minds of the men of Athens and Rome, the Middle Ages and the Renaissance, all of whom with varying degrees of accurate knowledge looked back to him as the Father of Song, the greatest of the ancient Bards who sang of heroes, gods and men.

From the time of the earliest critical literature, Homer is a figure to be reverenced for his divine gift. Although Plato is forced in the *Republic* to exclude some of the Homeric tales from his ideal city, it is clearly with a feeling of regret that he must turn his back upon the teacher who formed his mind in his youth. Aristotle, in the *Poetics,* takes Homer for granted as the greatest of the epic poets, and Aeschylus, the first of the great Athenian dramatists, deprecates his own productions as merely crumbs from the banquet table of Homer.

Homer's two great works are the *Iliad* and the *Odyssey.* The former tells the tale of the Trojan War, fought by the Greeks who sailed in their thousand ships against the enemy to bring back Helen, the wife of Menelaus, from the court of Paris, son of Priam. The *Odyssey* recounts the adventures of Odysseus, who, at the conclusion of the Trojan strife, becomes the plaything of gods and goddesses and has his return home delayed for ten more years. Meanwhile his sorrowing wife and growing son look forward to his return in hopeless longing. In ancient Greece these Homeric tales were the fundamental of all education; in translations, his heroes have nourished the imaginations of all times and nations. Homer has been the teacher and textbook of life for countless generations of mankind.

It remained for the critics of the eighteenth century, however, to mar the illusions of so many centuries. A meticulous examination of the style and content of the Homeric Poems made general the opinion that no one man was the author of the *Iliad* and the *Odyssey*. A succession of separate writers, over a long period of time, it was concluded, took the various threads and themes, sagas and incidents from fact and fancy, and by an almost automatic process there arose the complete poems that have been known in their present form since the beginning of literary records in the West. The personality of Homer then became a mere fiction, and it was for a time distinctly unfashionable to speak of Homer as the author of the epic poems of Greece.

For the purposes of readers of the Great Books, however, it is of little importance whether Homer was one man or twenty; the significant thing is that these two poems have been known and loved and have exercised their influence on the formation of all of Western literature. The stories themselves are what really matter; the author, or authors, would be content with the anonymity maintained all through the poems, content to sing the lays of ancient times and to bring to the modern world a picture of the giants who lived in the times of Agamemnon.

For the *Odyssey* is truly a Great Book. Never in all literature has the art of epic narrative been brought to so successful a consummation as in the tale of the wanderings of the "wily Odysseus." Let us grant that a number of ancient stories were woven together into a unit which centers on the return of Odysseus from the siege of Troy. But, whoever put the *Odyssey* into the form in which we have it, there is no doubt of the cunning arrangement of part with part that has resulted. According to the canons of epic poetry, we are plunged into the midst of the story; as the tale progresses, the background and antecedent happenings are woven into it by the epic technique of having a bard recount the famous exploits of the men who fought around the walls of Troy.

Nor is the *Odyssey* merely a bald tale of the wanderings of a weary hero. Gods and men, battles and shipwrecks, monsters and marvels are all clothed in the inimitable garb of the author's imagination, and scenes from the story come alive in the minds of countless readers. Truly immortal are the pictures of the homesick Odysseus sitting amid the splendors of Calypso's island, longing to see the smoke rising into the morning air of his native land; of the tearful Penelope, weaving and unweaving the shroud of old Laertes in her loneliness; of the youthful Telemachus, standing before the council of Ithaca for the first time and demanding that his mother's pestilential suitors depart from his house. Homer's imagination soars to its greatest heights in the description of the furious storm that lashes the raft of Odysseus; equally terrifying are the adventures of his ship as it tries to cleave its way between the twin dangers of Scylla and Charybdis.

But, beyond these artistic qualities, it is the sheer humanity of Homer's tale that has won it so many admirers; in the person of Odysseus, men have seen the archetype of wandering mankind and an example of the dangers and pitfalls that await the weary and the weak. Memorable are the descriptions of the faithful wife, all but widowed by the long years of war; of the son who has been growing up in his father's absence, sorely missing the companionship, example and guidance of an older man; of wise old Nestor bowing his head in sadness when he can tell the son no news of his missing father.

Throughout the *Odyssey* we are presented with a picture of human nature in its pain and pathos, fidelity and chicanery, manifesting the height of Homeric morality and the crudeness of primitive justice and cruelty. For depth and truth of portrayal of elemental human nature, Homer has hardly been equaled in all literature.

Strangely enough for an epic of primitive society, the *Odyssey* abounds in beautiful descriptions of womanhood, which have become traditional symbols of their class. Apart from Penelope, there is the faithful old servant, Eurycleia, who finally recognizes Odysseus beneath his beggar's rags when she notices the scar on his leg, caused by a hunting accident in his youth. Then there is the chaste and somewhat coy Nausicaa, daughter of the Phaeacian king, who finds the sea-tossed wanderer on the shore where he has fallen in exhaustion. While her companions scream and run in terror from the horrible sight, Nausicaa is calm, commanding and in full control. She arranges everything with due regard for the demands of hospitality, good judgment and public opinion. Added to these, we have the distinctly feminine, if not more attractive, characters of Circe, Calypso, the Sirens and the wanton slave girls in the halls at Ithaca, grown bold and insolent during the confusion and encouraged by the suitors for the hand of their lady. So striking is this element in the *Odyssey* that one modern writer has tried to prove that the author of the poem was a woman.

No more than an outline of the diversified elements of the tale can here be given. The story opens when nearly twenty years have passed since the hero sailed away from his young bride. Their son is now almost come to man's estate. The Trojan War has been over for nearly ten years, and there has been no word from Odysseus; the young men of Ithaca and the surrounding islands of Dulichium and Zacynthus have moved into the house of the supposed widow, demanding that she make her choice of one of them and marry again. With no man in the house to control them, they do as they please, eating, drinking and carousing; they are devouring the substance of the absent hero. At the same time they corrupt the servants and insult the lady of the house. To forestall their demand, Penelope has agreed that she will marry but not until she has finished the funeral shroud of her father-in-law, Laertes. By night she unravels what she has woven by day. The trick is discovered and the suitors become more insistent.

At this point Telemachus decides to go to the aged Nestor at Pylos and to Sparta, the home of Menelaus, to seek information about his father. He gets away, evading by the help of the gods the ambush the suitors had laid for him, but his quest is all in vain since no one knows anything of Odysseus. Meanwhile the story shifts to the island where Odysseus is the unwilling captive of the goddess Calypso. As a reward for his love she has promised him wealth and immortality, but she has never stilled his longing for his home and family. Now, at last, she is commanded by a messenger of the gods to let him go. She provides him with materials for a raft, which he cunningly constructs, but he is no sooner on the high seas than his old enemy Poseidon sends a fearful storm. More dead than alive, he is tossed on the shore of Phaeacia. Brought to the palace of Alcinous by the prudent Nausicaa, he is received with all the propriety of ancient hospitality, clothed in fine robes, fed and entertained. Demodocus, the minstrel, sings of the heroes of Troy to the accompaniment of his lyre, and when he recalls the exploits of Odysseus (who has not been asked to identify himself), the hero covers his face with his cloak so that no one may see the tears that rise to his eyes. The king alone notices this, but with wonted Phaeacian delicacy he refrains from any questioning and bids the minstrel put an end to his song.

Next are arranged a series of games and races for the entertainment of the stranger. After the young men of Phaeacia have engaged in various contests of running, jumping and boxing, one of the princes taunts Odysseus. He does not look very strong, is the slur, and is probably a merchant and no athlete. Angered at this insult, Odysseus pleads exhaustion from his shipwreck, but without removing his cloak he grasps the heaviest discus there and throws it farther than any of the Phaeacian youths had been able to do—so far beyond the rest that an onlooker remarks dryly that even a blind man would be able to find that mark.

There follows a banquet, at which he finally tells his story. "I am Odysseus, son of Laertes, known among men, and the fame of my wisdom has spread over all the world." He goes on to tell of the loss of all of his companions on the voyage back from Troy; some fell in battle with the Ciconians; only by force was he able to drag them away from the land of the Lotus Eaters, tor any man who tastes that food wants to remain in that land forever; more were lost in the dreadful adventure with the one-eyed giant, Polyphemus, who locked them in a cave. But Odysseus, ever resourceful, put out the eye of the giant while he lay in a drunken stupor. When the stone sealing the cave was removed, he and his companions got out by clinging to the underside of the heavy fleece of the giant's sheep, while the blind monster felt their backs in vain.

Further storms delayed their return, and then they came to the land of the sorceress, Circe, who with magic potions could turn men into animals. Odysseus had been warned by Hermes and provided with an antidote which made him immune to her charms. In spite of his pleas, however, he lost some more of his men to Circe.

In her parting words, Circe had advised him that he must visit Hades and speak with the old prophet Tiresias, who would tell him what lay before him on the journey homewards. He does so and meets the heroes who died at Troy, as well as his old mother. Having been forewarned by the prophet, he sets out once again on his travels. With his crew deafened by wax poured into their ears, he successfully gets past the rocks where the Sirens sing; he himself has been bound hand and foot to the mast of his ship—otherwise he would have been charmed by their song and lost his chance to return home. The sad adventure on the island of Thrinacia deprives him of more of his men, destroyed for killing the sacred cattle of the Sun. The rest are lost in the storm which destroys the ship. Odysseus alone is saved and, after tossing on the sea for ten days, lands on the island of Calypso. Thus ends his story.

In a mysterious ship of the Phaeacians he is transported back to Ithaca. There he meets the faithful swineherd, Eumaeus, who labors still, faithful to his master though saddened by the depredations of the suitors. Athena brings Telemachus back from his travels and Odysseus reveals himself to both. Plans are laid, and Odysseus goes to his own house in the guise of a beggar; he is recognized by Eurycleia, strips the hall of all weapons and then provokes a contest with his own ponderous bow and arrow; when no one can bend the bow, Odysseus, ignoring the scornful laughter of the suitors, takes it in his hands and sends the arrow winging to the target. Before the suitors can recover from their amazement, he turns on them and they are all slaughtered at the banquet tables. The unfaithful servants are likewise sent to their fate, and soon the time has come to reveal to Penelope that she is at last free of the suitors and that her husband is home. The story ends with a banquet which celebrates the joy of all the family at their happy reunion.

Discussion of the *Odyssey* is particularly fruitful in the analysis of character, in which Homer was a master. The clear-cut motivations of all actions which move the story to its end constitute an illuminating commentary on Homeric morality and on the ideals of conduct which inspired that primitive society. The inevitable shortcomings of these ideals will be clear in the light of Christian civilization, but the conclusion is inescapable that the natural virtues truly flourished in Homeric times. Homer's narrative and dramatic technique will be of interest to those who read the *Poetics* of Aristotle and the dramatic works which depended on Homer for their themes and their basic characterization. But, apart from such utilitarian elements, it will be a truly great human experience to have lived for a time with the man who says, in Tennyson's poem:

I am become a name;
For always roaming with a hungry heart
Much have I seen and known; cities of men
And manners, climates, councils, governments,
Myself not least, but honored of them all;
And drunk delight of battle with my peers,
Far on the ringing plains of windy Troy;
I am part of all that I have met.

EDWIN A. QUAIN

SELECTED BIBLIOGRAPHY

BUTCHER and LANG, *The Odyssey*. Macmillan.
BASSETT, Samuel E., *The Poetry of Homer*. University of California.
SCOTT, John A., *The Unity of Homer*. University of California.
WOODHOUSE, William J., *The Composition of Homer's Odyssey*. Oxford.
HOMER, *The Odyssey*. Random (Modern Library).
HOMER, *Odyssey*. Regnery.
HOMER, *The Odyssey*. Dutton (Everyman's Library).

Herodotus: History, *Books I and II*

FROM THE MIDDLE of the eighth to the middle of the sixth century B.C. a great economic development, beginning in Greek Ionia on the west coast of Asia Minor and spreading to the maritime cities on the Greek mainland, brought about a remarkable expansion of the Greeks, an expansion which sent them to almost every shore of the Mediterranean as well as to the Black Sea. Though at first this expansion, or colonization, was motivated by the need of raw materials for Greek industry and of outlets for their finished products, it finally led to other, more far-reaching results. As the Greeks observed in their travels through the world the diversity of ideas and customs among different peoples, their natural disposition (and of the Ionians in particular) for exploring everything within the sphere of human interest received its strongest impetus, making them the pioneers of our Western civilization. It was in this way that the Greeks became the creators not only of philosophy but also of historiography, that is, the art of writing history.

Though we find collections of historical material—records of chroniclers and lists of rulers—among nations of the ancient Near East at an earlier date, historical thinking could develop only where free nations, with a natural instinct and feeling for the great achievements of their history, produced men freed from the restrictions of mythological traditions, who reported only those things capable of standing the test of man's critical intellect. As a matter of fact, among those Near Eastern nations, the Hebrews were the only ones who produced genuine historical works at a very early time. What is more, these works—the historical books of the Old Testament—show outstanding qualities: emphasis is laid on the unity of the human race and its common goal; there is a striving after impartiality and objectivity of judgment, and a lively and reverent interest in the past of their nation.

However, it is not to the Hebrews that Western civilization owes the literary form of historiography, but to the inquiring mind of the Greeks, who speculated on everything under the sun and sought the root and reason of historical events. Thus, when the Romans began to write their history, they did so after the Greek fashion; and in the *Ecclesiastical History* of Eusebius of Caesarea, the first Church historian, we note that the spirit with which he outlines the plan of his work is identical with that which characterizes the historical ideal of the Greeks.

The Greek word *historia,* from which our word "history" is derived, originally meant inquiry, research, learning or knowing by inquiry. It is in this sense that Herodotus uses the word in the very first line of his great work, *The Persian Wars.* "This," he writes, "is a presentation of the researches of Herodotus of Halicarnassus." The Greek historians had for their object the satisfying of man's inquiry into the actions of his fellow man, and thus it comes about that, among the peoples of our Western civilization, it was the Greeks who first cultivated history for its own sake, for the love of historical truth.

Cicero called Herodotus the "Father of History." This statement demands some qualification. Herodotus is not the first but the last in a long series of writers who, with the help of rational criticism, attempted to purge the old epic tales of elements contrary to nature, and of miracle stories about gods and demigod heroes, thus molding legendary traditions into a credible history of early Greece. By common consent these pre-Herodotean writers of chronicles have become known as *logographoi* (writers of *logoi* or prose compositions). Their attempts at systemization and criticism are naïve, and they still consider Homer and the other epic poets trustworthy authorities for early Greek history. Yet they can claim the credit of having made an honest effort to distinguish myth from fact, to look for rational explanations for causes and effects, and to replace mythical tales by real genealogies and secular records of their city-states.

Their attitude can best be described by quoting a fragment of the *Genealogiai* of Hecateus of Miletus (ca. 500 B. C.), the outstanding early logographer: "I write what I consider to be the truth; for the traditions of the Greeks seem to me many and ridiculous." In antiquity, geography was closely connected with historiography—witness the numerous geographical excursuses we find in the works of ancient historians. Thus Hecateus also wrote, besides his historical work, one on geography, entitled "Travels around the Earth," in two books—one on Europe, the other on Asia, the latter giving also a comprehensive account of Egypt. Not only history and geography but also ethnology played a large part in the works of pre-Herodotean writers. They gave descriptions of the character, homes, habits and institutions of the different peoples and the climate of their countries. From the fragments which have come down to us we can reasonably conclude that their purpose was to entertain their audience and satisfy their curiosity.

It was in possession of this cultural inheritance that Herodotus set out on his quest after historical truth. Many passages in his work, his narrative style and particularly the main structure of the earlier books indicate that he began in the tradition of his predecessors. That he became an historian in a new and higher sense of the word, as did so many after him, was due to his realization of the momentous significance of the Persian Wars, which saved Greece from becoming a Persian satrapy of the Asiatic type.

This discovery changed his entire outlook. History was no longer to him, as it was to his predecessors, a mere sequence of isolated, unconnected episodes but an undivided, coherent whole. In a magnificent conception, comparable to St. Augustine's antithesis of the "City of God" and the "Terrestrial City," he reorganized his material under the aspect of a coherent struggle between the Hellenes and the Barbarians, between Asia and Europe, a struggle in which the intellectual and spiritual power of small liberty-loving Greece triumphed over Asiatic despotism, with its brutal force and numerical superiority. This struggle became the central theme of his work. Though often, especially in the first part, he went into lengthy digressions, he never lost sight of the general plan.

To understand the influence of his predecessors as well as the importance of his innovation we must turn to what can be learned of Herodotus' life. He was born at Halicarnassus, a Greek city on the west coast of Asia Minor, about 484 B.C., only six years after the sea-borne invasion of central Greece by Darius had ended in a Persian defeat at Marathon, and four years before the battles of Thermopylae and Salamis. Exiled from his native town, he settled first at Samos, then at Athens, and later at Thurii, the Panhellenic colony founded by Pericles in Magna Graecia, the group of Greek colonies along the coast of southern Italy. The last years of his life were probably spent again in Athens.

In between, he undertook extensive journeys, collecting, as did his predecessor Hecateus, a great wealth of information concerning the countries and peoples he visited. These travels brought him not only to the mainland of Greece and its islands, to Macedonia, Thrace, and Magna Graecia, but also through Asia Minor, Assyria, and Babylonia as far as Susa and Ecbatana. In the north, he went as far as the north coast of the Black Sea; in the south, he journeyed through Egypt as far as the first cataract and also visited Cyrene on the coast of North Africa.

These travels were of great importance for Herodotus' growth and development as an historian. They made him recognize the true magnitude of the peril the Greeks had escaped, and the momentous consequences of their victorious struggle for political freedom. As a result, he gave a new interpretation of the great events of the immediate past, presenting the Persian Wars as a phase of the eternal conflict between East and West. It was the choice of subject and this entirely new manner of interpreting and presenting historical events, that raised Herodotus far above his predecessors and made him the first real historian of our Western civilization.

Besides attaining for the first time the stable aspect of the historical ideal, namely, the conservation of historical facts for their own sake, Herodotus distinguished himself by still another characteristic quality of the true historian. In spite of his sincere admiration for the great achievements of the Greeks, and of the Athenians in particular, he never became narrow in his views, but made an honest effort to do justice to Greece's opponents. He found, for instance, words of high praise for the valor of the Persians, their veracity, their loyalty to their royal house, and for a great number of their customs and institutions. His Croesus and Darius are sympathetic figures. Though a firm supporter of democratic institutions, he did not shut his eyes to the political shortcomings of the Greeks, and he showed his impartiality by condemning the errors of some democratic leaders and acknowledging the merits of some oligarchs and Oriental despots.

To be sure, some parts of Herodotus' work seem to be out of proportion and to lack the proper relation to the main theme. However, such minor blemishes should not be overstated, for he evidently tried several different approaches to his subject before he decided on its basic structure. Indeed, considerable portions were written before the final plan was chosen. Herodotus died (ca. 425 B.C.) before he could complete and systematically revise his work. That he devoted almost half his work to the histories of Lydia, Egypt and the Persian Empire was due to his endeavor to render his account as complete as possible.

In this way his work also became a kind of "universal history," going beyond the more limited scope of a national history. As to the many digressions and the insertion of numerous tales, we must not forget that he was still in the tradition of that literary technique which his predecessors had taken over from the epic poets. The fictional material so profusely inserted into an historical narrative may drive a pragmatic historian to despair, but it is futile to expect too rigorous methods of historiography from Herodotus, who lived in a time of transition.

We may add that the tales of Herodotus differ from the epic poems insofar as they are not myths in the strict sense of the word, but novels. It is typical of the Greek world that its great personalities lived on in short novels whose subject was the solution of problems. Herodotus' novel of Periander and his son, for instance, deals with the problem of a son's attitude toward his father, who has slain the son's mother. The Egyptian tales in Book II have a didactic character. We have, for example, the story of King Amasis, whose subjects looked down on him as having come from an undistinguished house. The king caused a golden foot-pan to be converted into an idol, which the people promptly worshiped with the utmost veneration. The king now pointed out the unimportance of antecedents and thus won the respect of the people.

Herodotus got these tales from the natives as he, a foreigner, understood them. It is not very often that he tells what his reasons were for accepting or rejecting something he had heard. More often he admits he cannot be sure of the truth because conflicting accounts were offered. On the whole, the accounts which he offers without expressing any critical opinion far outnumber those which he doubts or refuses to believe. However, his general attitude toward them can be seen from his statement, "For myself, my duty is to tell what is reported, but I am not obliged to believe it all alike, and let this remark be applied to every narrative in my History." However this may be, we cannot expect his standards to be the same as those of the twentieth century.

The division into nine books, in accordance with the number of the Muses, belongs to a later period and may have been the work of one of the great Alexandrian scholars, perhaps Aristarchus of Samothrace (220-143 B.C.), who wrote a commentary to Herodotus. Of these nine books the first two have been chosen as a Great Book. They give us a particular insight into the author's outlook on history, his interpretation of facts, and his literary technique.

In the short Preface, Herodotus describes the purpose of his *History:* "that time may not blot out the great deeds of the Hellenes and the Barbarians, and especially that the causes for which they waged war with one another may not be forgotten." Note that here we have for the first time the recording of historical facts for their own sake and a desire to be unbiased toward either side.

Though, in the first chapters of Book I, the abductions of Io, Europa and Helena are mentioned as causes of the ill feeling between the Hellenes and the Asiatic peoples, Herodotus himself considers the conquest of Greek cities in Asia Minor by the kings of Lydia the first real and historical cause of the hostilities. This leads him to give an account of the history of the Lydian monarchy since Gyges, with special emphasis on the reign of the last Lydian king, Croesus, who succumbed to the power of the Persian Cyrus in 546 B.C. The mention of Croesus's relations with the oracle of Delphi gives the author an opportunity to insert some important portions of the history of Athens and Sparta.

After treating the conquest of Lydia by Cyrus, Herodotus describes the beginnings of the Persian Empire established by Cyrus, then the earlier Eastern empires, the Assyrian, Babylonian and Median, from the last of which rose the Persian. The customs and domestic affairs of the Persian realm are described at full length. Herodotus also gives an exhaustive account of the three main campaigns of Cyrus: the campaign against the Asiatic Greeks who were overcome; the capture of Babylon, which gives Herodotus an opportunity to describe the marvels of that great and splendid city; the campaign against the Massagetae, whose invasion of eastern Iran about 530 B.C. cost Cyrus his life.

Cyrus's successor on the Persian throne was his son Cambyses, whose conquest of Egypt in 525 B.C. rounded out the Persian Empire to include the whole civilized East from the Nile Delta eastward almost to India. The Egyptian campaign induces Herodotus to devote the entire second book to a description of the wonderland on the Nile, whose gigantic monuments had made a deep impression on the open-minded Greek traveler. Special attention is given to the religious ideas and customs of the Egyptians.

In order to show the relation of the first two books to the whole work, a short outline of the remaining books is here given. In Book III Herodotus resumes the history of Persia, giving an account of the conquest of Egypt, Libya and Cyrene, the death of Cambyses (522 B.C.), the reign of the usurper Smerdis, the conspiracy of the Persian nobles against the Magi, and the accession of Darius I, the third Persian conqueror, to the throne. There is added a concise account of the organization of the Persian Empire into satrapies, or provinces, its excellent system of taxation and its enormous resources. This also serves to show how formidable an enemy small Greece had to face.

Book IV deals with the campaign of Darius against the Scythians on the Lower Danube, Dnieper and Don. This offers an opportunity for describing the country, manners and customs not only of the Scythians but also of the other peoples in northeastern Europe. The plan of the Persians to conquer also the narrow strip of fertile land along the north shore of Africa, leads the author to give an account of the Greek colonies in Libya, especially Cyrene, and the manners and customs of its inhabitants.

Book V begins with the Persians gaining the first foothold on the European continent by making Thrace a Persian satrapy, and contains chiefly the history of the Ionian revolt which, ill advised, ill prepared and lacking the necessary unity, ended in failure (494 B.C.) and brought the struggle between the Hellenes and the Persians into a new phase. Since Aristagoras of Miletus, the most active leader of the revolt against the Persians, went to Sparta and Athens to enlist their aid, Herodotus can resume here the history of the Greek states where he left off in the first book, describing especially the rapid rise of Athens under the Pisistratidae.

Book VI describes Darius's further attempts at absorbing the Balkan peninsula into his realm. The flight of the Spartan king Demaratus to Darius is used to insert an account of the quarrels of the Greek city-states engrossed in their own particularist interests and blind to the enormous danger threatening them. The book closes with the Athenian victory at Marathon (490 B.C.).

Books VII, VIII and IX contain a minute description of the campaign of the fourth Persian conqueror, Xerxes, against the Greek motherland. The highlights of the vivid account are the battle of Thermopylae, the naval engagement at the promontory at Artemisium, the capture of Athens with the burning of the Acropolis, the naval victory at Salamis, the end of the great war on Greek soil by the Persian defeat at Plataea (479 B.C.), and the liberation of the Ionian cities from Persian rule by a naval victory off the coast of Mycale. The leading figures in the Greek War of Independence, Leonidas, Aristides, Themistocles, are portrayed with great warmth of feeling. The last event mentioned by Herodotus is the capture of Sestus on the European side of the Hellespont (478 B.C.). He concludes his work by giving a short retrospect of Cyrus and the formidable Persian war power, which succumbed to the free men of Hellas defending their autonomy.

Thus, in spite of the many digressions, the work possesses an artistic unity which is further strengthened by the author's personal outlook on the world and on history. The narrative is held together by the one basic idea that history is the result of an eternal moral law governing the fate of man. This law, established by the deity, sets limits to man, showing him his dependency on the deity and the instability of all things earthly. If man in wanton presumption transgresses these limits, rashly disturbing the equilibrium of the moral world, established and maintained by the deity, either he or his descendants will feel the righteous anger of the gods. Herodotus sees especially in the outcome of the Persian Wars an ordeal ordained by the deity.

Herodotus has often been censured for his deficiencies of historical technique, especially by nineteenth-century critics proud of their achievements in developing the critical method of historical research. However, the blame for this must be attributed, at least in part, to the fact that Herodotus lived in a time when the Greeks had just begun to take a critical attitude toward their early history. On the other hand, undeniably great achievements compensate for these shortcomings. First of all, Herodotus is our chief authority for Greek, Lydian, Persian and Egyptian history of the sixth century B.C. and the first twenty years of the fifth. Moreover, he has supplied anthropologists, sociologists and historians of religions with material of great importance. The many tales he inserted are a valuable contribution to cultural history, in which Herodotus showed a lively interest. The fact that he was the first historian of our Western civilization to give one great, basic idea to a sum of historical occurrences has already been mentioned. Not least in importance is the charm of Herodotus' literary style, which has made him one of the outstanding narrators in the world's great literature.

RUDOLPH ARBESMANN

SELECTED BIBLIOGRAPHY

BURY, J. B., *The Ancient Greek Historians* (Harvard Lectures). Macmillan.
GLOVER, T. R., *Herodotus*. University of California.
MARTIN, Ch. B., *Herodotus* (Martin Classical Lectures, Vol. I). Harvard University.
PEARSON, L., *Early Ionian Historians*. Oxford (The Clarendon Press).
HERODOTUS, *History*. Dutton (Everyman's Library).
HERODOTUS, *History*, Books I and II. Regnery.

Aeschylus: House of Atreus (*Agamemnon,*
The Choephori, The Eumenides)

THE GREEK word "drama" means action. It is not just a story
whose characters are described in a narrative form—this would
be an epic. It is rather a story enacted before the eyes of the
spectators who have come to the theatre, "the seeing-place." The
characters of the story are represented by actors who imitate them
in voice, manners, gestures, dress and actions. In his *Poetics,*
Aristotle says that "imitation is natural to man from his childhood" and that "it is also natural for all to delight in the works
of imitation." The natural desire of man to leave the never-
changing pace of everyday life, to slip into the mask of another
person, to be someone else, is a basic root of dramatic art.

Though the earliest history of Greek dramatic art is obscure
and subject to conjecture, its development may have taken place
somewhat as follows. It had its origin in religion, growing up
gradually from a ritual in honor of Dionysus, the god of vegetation. Each spring at the time of the great Dionysiac Festivals, the
god was thought to arrive from overseas to revive vegetation.
In the person of his priest, he was brought in a wagon disguised
as a ship through Athens to the sacred precincts of his temple on
the south side of the Acropolis. He was accompanied by a chorus
of singers who, as satyrs, were dressed in goatskins and sometimes
spoken of simply as goats (*tragoi*). Hence, the hymn they sang in
honor of Dionysus was called "tragedy," which means "goat
song." In the course of time, the chorus leader began to imper-
sonate a character in the song, and the theme of the hymn could
be taken from another story than that of Dionysus. For instance,
the chorus leader and his singers could enact, in a primitive
fashion, the story of a hero's conflict with his enemies.

Out of these rude dramatic or quasi-dramatic attempts there grew up that immortal art which we admire in the extant plays of Aeschylus, Sophocles and Euripides, who wrote in the fifth century B.C. We owe the preservation of these plays to the scholars of Alexandria who singled them out because of their excellence; the works of their less important competitors have been lost. With Aeschylus, then, the earliest of the three, we are on safe ground in the history of the Greek drama and at its very height. We have before us the finished product of a long dramatic, or at least quasi-dramatic, tradition, which we are able to reconstruct only in a theoretical and conjectural way.

Aeschylus, for good reasons, has been called the Father of Tragedy. In his *Poetics,* Aristotle attributes to him the addition of a second actor to the first, the latter having been introduced by Thespis (ca. 534 B.C.). Such minor characters as soldiers, attendants, etc. were not counted as actors. He also restricted the choral parts, thus making of the dialog, or spoken portion, the most important part in the play. The importance of these innovations is obvious. Now the dialog could develop far more freely than when it existed only between the leader of the chorus and one actor. It is through the dialog that the action, the essential element of drama, comes to the forefront and moves irresistibly forward toward the solution, the end. We are able to follow the poet's steady growth in technical ability. In an early play, *The Suppliants,* the chorus still figures large, but the plays of his *Oresteia* trilogy show a fully developed dramaturgy. The original chorus drama has become an actor drama. Aeschylus also developed an interconnection between dialog and chorus, so that both together formed a logical whole. He is credited, too, with scenic innovations, such as scene painting and mechanical devices.

Aeschylus, the son of a prominent landowner of Eleusis, an old Attic city, was born in 525 B.C. Nothing is known concerning his education. The remark of Sophocles that Aeschylus did the right thing unconsciously, refers to his extraordinarily gifted disposition, his genius, and not to a possible lack of training. The account of his entering into friendly relations with Pindar may be correct, although the statement that Pindar had learned from him looks rather like an invention of local Attic patriotism. That he was acquainted with the poems of Homer, the other poets of the epic cycle and Hesiod is evident from the themes of his

dramas. He also was influenced by the choral lyric of Archilo-
chus, Alcaeus and Anacreon. But it is the spirit of Solon and the
latter's firm belief that all human activity is subject to the ordinances of *Dikē*, Justice, a personification of man's moral conscience, that is most important in Aeschylus' outlook on the
world.

As far as we can see, he was a supporter of the democratic
principle, although, in his conception, this did not exclude the
leadership of one man trusted by the people and conscious of
his great responsibility. Leaders of this kind are all the good
kings of his dramas. Though not a friend of war and internecine
feuds, he firmly believed in a democracy able to defend itself,
and he gave proof of his conviction by fighting in the great battles
of Marathon, Salamis and Plataea. The Athenian battle of Marathon, in which he was wounded, appeared to him the most important of all. His participation in that battle, and not his
poetical achievements, he considered worthy of being perpetuated
in the four lines of his self-composed epitaph. We do not know
whether he took an active part in politics, but his interest in
and attitude toward political questions are manifest in the seven
plays that have come down to us.

Aeschylus was a prolific writer, producing—we are told—some
ninety dramas. After having competed for the first time in the
dramatic contests of the year 499 B.C., he won the first prize in
488 B.C.—we do not know with what plays. After this victory he
dominated the Athenian stage for almost a generation. In 468
B.C. he lost the first prize to his young competitor Sophocles
but recaptured his position in 467 B.C. with a trilogy of which
only the third play, *The Seven against Thebes*, survived. In
458 B.C. he achieved his last and greatest triumph with the
Oresteia trilogy. At the zenith of his fame (about 474 B.C.) he
accepted an invitation of the Tyrant Hieron of Syracuse, the
great patron of arts and letters, and lived for a while at the
latter's magnificent court. After his last success on the stage, he
went a second time to Sicily and died there near Gela in 456 B.C.

Aeschylus' masterpiece, the *Oresteia*, has been chosen as a
Great Book. It is a series of three tragedies related in subject and
intended for consecutive performance. The individual titles of
the three plays are *Agamemnon*, *The Choephori* (named after
the chorus of the "Libation Bearers" who have accompanied

Agamemnon's daughter Electra to her father's tomb in the opening scene), and *The Eumenides* ("The Gracious Goddesses"),
which takes its name from the euphemistic, deprecatory appella-
tion given to the chorus of the Erinyes, or Furies.

The theme of the *Oresteia* is the workings of an hereditary
curse upon the members of the royal house of the Atridae, guilty
and innocent alike. It is based on the idea that violence once
committed by man's insolent pride and excess breeds new violence, driving his descendants, through generation after generation, to new transgressions and final destruction. The gods hear
the curse, and the one who has committed the first violence
cannot escape the eternal law of retribution—he is punished not
only in his own person but also in his descendants. In order to
understand the problem we must keep in mind that, in Greek
thought, the family is not merely a loose aggregation of parents,
children and grandchildren, but a sacred union and sequence of
blood, stretching from the remote past into the far future, bound
together by a continuity of inviolable obligations. Every trans-
gression of the moral law by a member of the family brings down
divine indignation upon the whole family.

The great example, treated by each of the greater dramatists
of Greece, is the story of the Tantalides, the descendants of the
Phrygian king Tantalus, who begot Pelops, who begot Atreus,
who begot Agamemnon, who begot Orestes. Tantalus is the first
of the race to commit an atrocious offense against the gods, who
have heaped benefits upon him. Recklessly proud of his wealth,
incapable of bearing his good fortune, he is led by Ate, blind
Folly, to steal the nectar and ambrosia of the gods and to give the
divine food to his son Pelops. Coming to the western Pelopon-
nesus, Pelops aspires to the throne of Elis, attainable through
marriage to Hippodameia, daughter of King Oenomaus. The
latter is willing to give his daughter and kingdom to any suitor
capable of defeating him in a chariot race. A number of suitors
have tried and lost their lives. Pelops attains his end by foul
means. He bribes the king's charioteer, Myrtilus, to remove the
linch-pins of the royal chariot, promising him a share in the rule
of the state. Oenomaus is killed in the race, but Pelops also
eliminates his accomplice, who dies with an ominous curse upon
Pelops and all his descendants.

The chain of crimes continues with the sons of Pelops, Atreus and Thyestes. Thyestes seduces Aerope, the wife of Atreus; the latter kills the sons of Thyestes and serves them in a banquet to their father. Thyestes curses the house of Atreus, who has two sons, Agamemnon and Menelaus, the Atridae. Agamemnon marries Clytaemnestra, by whom he has two daughters, Iphigenia and Electra, and one son, Orestes. Setting out for Troy, Agamemnon is detained by a windless sea at Aulis and sacrifices Iphigenia to obtain favorable winds. Angered by the loss of her daughter, Clytaemnestra, in the absence of her husband, takes as her lover Aegisthus, Thyestes' sole surviving son, who burns with a desire to wreak his vengeance upon the house of the Atridae. He and Clytaemnestra conspire to kill Agamemnon on his return after the capture of Troy. It is at this point that Aeschylus takes up the tale of the curse.

The *Agamemnon* opens with the arrival of the news of Troy's capture and the reaction it produces in the royal palace in Argos. Then Agamemnon himself arrives, escorted by his victorious troops, and receives a lavish welcome from his wife Clytaemnestra. In his company there is Cassandra, a Trojan princess and prophetess, who, in the distribution of the booty, has fallen to the king's lot. In a stirring scene she predicts approaching disaster and her own death. Soon the audience hears the death cry of Agamemnon, who has been slain by his wife and her paramour. The central doors of the palace open. Clytaemnestra comes forward in wild triumph, ax in hand and blood on her forehead, glorying in her deed and defending her right to have committed the murder. In the background lie the bodies of Agamemnon and Cassandra. The play closes with Aegisthus announcing that he has taken possession of throne and country, and the leader of the chorus uttering the ominous warning that "a deity might guide Orestes safely on his way home."

In the second play of the trilogy, *The Choephori*, we witness how Orestes, Agamemnon's son and heir, avenges his father's murder. Apollo, the god in special charge of expiation for bloodshed, drives him to perform his duty according to the decrees of ancestral law which put the punishment of murder on the dead man's next of kin. Clytaemnestra has sent her son to far-off Phocis so that he may forget his father's death. Orestes, however, comes to Argos secretly with his companion Pylades. When they are at Agamemnon's tomb, a procession of slave women bearing vessels for libation (the chorus of the Libation Bearers), slowly approaches the monument, followed by Orestes' sister, Electra. The friends withdraw and Orestes hears the girl call upon her father's spirit to arouse his son to avenge him. Thereupon Orestes reveals himself to his sister, who pours out to him all the bitterness she feels for their mother. He acquaints her with his plan. He and Pylades, disguised as travelers from Phocis, call at the palace, where they are hospitably received by Clytaemnestra. In the course of conversation Orestes tells the queen that Agamemnon's heir, the avenger she and Aegisthus have to fear, is no more. Though feigning deep grief, Clytaemnestra's heart rejoices, and she calls Aegisthus to hear the good news. The hour of revenge has come. Orestes slays Aegisthus and drives his mother into the palace before him. But no sooner has he shed her blood, than he comes out, driven mad by the realization that he is a matricide.

In the third play, *The Eumenides,* Orestes, pursued by the Erinyes, or Furies, personifications of man's moral conscience, flees to Delphi to find a haven of rest at the altar of Apollo, at whose command he has avenged his father. The chorus of the Furies, horrible to behold, has been lulled to sleep and lies nearby. Apollo, the god of purifications and expiations, leads the youth through their midst and on to Athens. There, through the intervention of the goddess Athena, Orestes' case is tried before the renowned Council of the Areopagus, presided over by the goddess herself.

This scene in the supreme court of justice in Athens, with the Erinyes acting as prosecutors and Apollo as counsel for the defendant, is of great symbolical importance. It is not Orestes alone who is judged; the verdict applies to all similar offenders in the future. The state—represented as a moral power—no longer leaves the right of punishment to the next of kin but takes upon itself the duty of prosecution. The court is equally divided and so Athena casts the deciding ballot in favor of Orestes, who is acquitted. She appeases the disappointed Erinyes by establishing their cult on the hill of Ares where the highest judicial court will deal with murder and other capital crimes in the future.

In studying the phenomenon of an ancestral curse, of sin begetting sin, Aeschylus attacks a problem which has always preoccupied the minds of men—the existence of evil in the world. He finds the solution of this problem in man's humble acknowledgment of a moral order which comes from above and resolves the discords of earthly life not only by punishing unrelentingly all outbursts of human passion but also by taking under its protection everyone who respectfully returns within his proper bounds.

In the *Oresteia*, Apollo appears not only as the inexorable avenger of bloodguilt but also as the savior who leads man out of a labyrinth of crimes from which no escape seems possible. Aeschylus is the first to express in precise terms the idea of the salutary effect of heaven-sent, undeserved suffering, which man should bear with resignation to a higher will and gratefully accept as a means of moral improvement. "Wisdom learned by suffering"—these simple but profound words represent enormous progress when compared with the old Greek saying that bold venture includes suffering, or with the fatalistic conception of a mechanical sequence of good and ill fortune. By taking a positive attitude toward the problem of suffering, by substituting teleology for purely mechanical causality, that is, by asserting that suffering has to fulfil a higher final end, the poet has found the key to a new, deeply religious solution of the tragic problem.

He did not exploit his discovery further for artistic purposes. Nor did Sophocles develop the idea, still less Euripides. It is found, however, in the writings of Plato; Herodotus, too, puts the Aeschylean doctrine into the mouth of his King Croesus.

Aeschylus' basic orientation, then, is toward religion. Witness the boundless confidence of Orestes in the god Apollo, who has promised him, "I desert thee never." Witness also the choral songs with their ardent plea for a religion of forgiveness. Witness, finally, the poet's attempt to reach beyond polytheism to the conception of one God Who is the supreme upholder of the moral order in the world. The great opening choral ode of the *Agamemnon* is a magnificent hymn in praise of the world-embracing power and rule of Zeus, who teaches man moderation, forewarns him and leads him to true wisdom through suffering. Agamemnon does not heed Zeus's warnings nor learn by heaven-sent suffering. This is his tragic guilt, which causes his final destruction.

The *leitmotif* just described recurs in the other choral passages of the *Agamemnon*, though the poet's interpretation seems to stress the idea that God's justice works according to the principle of "an eye for an eye." Also at the close of *The Choephori* it looks as if Clytaemnestra's murder of her husband is expiated by a matricide. The final solution is given in *The Eumenides*. Though Orestes has acted by order of Apollo, he has violated the "unwritten laws" which command piety toward the parents. Thus the only possible solution consists in tempering justice with mercy. Orestes is freed because he has become "perfect by suffering." Aeschylus closes the trilogy by repeating his conception of the godhead, which is at once just and merciful.

A closing remark may serve to complete the picture we have given of Aeschylus. His power of characterization is not inferior to his art of dramatic construction. This is apparent especially in *The Choephori,* where the poet places the action in the very soul of Orestes, whose pangs of conscience are the pivots of the tragedy. Orestes is not impelled by unavoidable fate but struggles through to freedom of decision and action and is transformed from a mere youth into a man by the superhuman task placed upon his shoulders. Thus the actor carries forward the unfolding of the plot; and though the last play, *The Eumenides,* displays once again the whole power and majesty of the chorus, whose lyrical and musical moods made it the matrix of the ancient art of tragedy, the main attention is no longer centered in the chorus, as in Aeschylus' early plays, but in the chief hero, Orestes.

RUDOLPH ARBESMANN

SELECTED BIBLIOGRAPHY

HAMILTON, E., *The Greek Way*. Norton.
MURRAY, G., *Aeschylus, the Creator of Tragedy*. Oxford (The Clarendon Press).
SHEPPARD, J. T., *Aeschylus and Sophocles, Their Work and Influence*. Longmans, Green.
SMYTH, H. W., *Aeschylean Tragedy*. University of California.
THOMSON, G. D., *Aeschylus and Athens, a Study in the Social Origins of Drama*. London: Lawrence & Wishart.
AESCHYLUS, *Dramas*. Dutton (Everyman's Library).
AESCHYLUS, *House of Atreus (Agamemnon, Libation Bearers, Furies)*. Regnery.

Sophocles: Oedipus Rex, Antigone

THE LATERAN MUSEUM at Rome contains one of the most beautiful ancient portrait statues in existence. It is the statue of a man standing erect in an easy attitude. The left hand rests on his hip, and the broad and lofty head is slightly lifted, showing gentle and imaginative eyes, a firm cheek, and a serious but benevolent mouth. The statue is an ideal picture of mental capacity and manly beauty, an example of perfect manhood. Found in 1838 at Terracina, a Latian town on the Appian Way south of Rome, it represents Sophocles who, together with Euripides, continued the work of Aeschylus, the Father of Greek tragedy. It is a marble copy. The original probably was one of the bronze statues of the three great tragic poets, which, at the instigation of the Athenian statesman Lycurgus, were placed in the Athenian theatre about 330 B.C.

Euripides (480-406 B.C.), the younger of the two successors of Aeschylus on the Athenian stage, was a man of brooding disposition who analyzed the actual feelings and motives of human beings facing the complex problems of life. Sophocles (496-406 B.C.) possessed both Aeschylus' lofty conception of a god-determined destiny in human life and Euripides' great gift of psychological analysis. The sculptor endeavored to portray the poet as a man who has attained the height of human excellence and happiness— a portrait which fits in with what we know of Sophocles' life.

A healthy, handsome youth, son of a rich sword manufacturer, he grew up at a time when Athens was leading the victorious struggle of the European Greeks for their liberty against the Persian lust for conquest. A skilled athlete and harpist, at sixteen he was chosen by the city to lead the chorus of boys who sang the paean of victory after the battle of Salamis (480 B.C.). He was a cheerful companion, and popular, and his poetic gift did not prevent him from being judicious and competent in managing a business. Thus his fellow citizens elected him to high offices in the democratic state. During 443-442 B.C. he was treasurer of the Confederate Fund of the Delian League which, in the course of time, had grown into an Athenian maritime empire. He even became one of the ten *strategoi,* or generals, who commanded the Athenian forces against Samos, which in 440 B.C. had seceded from the League and asked Persia for help. Though Pericles preferred Sophocles' poetry to his strategy, the campaign was successful and Samos was reduced after nearly a year's fighting.

The comic poet Phrynichus called Sophocles happy for not having been visited by any misfortunes during his life. Sophocles certainly was spared the grief of witnessing the fateful year 404 B.C., when Athens's enemies laid an iron ring around the city and starved the inhabitants into surrender. However, we know too little of Sophocles' personal life to be sure that Phrynichus' statement is correct. The poet's interpretation of life, as found in his tragedies, may have led to such utterances. But we should not forget that it must have been a deep experience of life which helped Sophocles to arrive at such a clear formulation. It must have been his personal attitude toward life which gave him the strength to overcome the forces which seem to have broken the spirit of his contemporary Euripides.

With Sophocles, Attic tragedy reached its perfection. He increased the number of actors to three. By this innovation he brought about a further restriction of the choral songs which, however, gained in depth of thought and feeling and in the melodious sound of their language and rhythm. In 468 B.C., a young man of twenty-eight, he gained his first victory over the older master Aeschylus. Of about one hundred twenty plays which he wrote, only seven tragedies have come down to us in their entirety. Of these, *Ajax, Philoctetes* and *Electra* belong to the Trojan Saga; *The Trachinae* to the Heracles Saga; *Oedipus Rex, Oedipus at Colonus* and *Antigone* to the Theban Saga.

Oedipus Rex and *Antigone* form the contents of a Great Book for modern reading and discussion. Though they and *Oedipus at Colonus* belong to the Theban Oedipus legend, they were produced separately and form only an unintentional trilogy. Sophocles broke with the tradition according to which the three tragedies, presented by a poet for the festival of the Greater Dionysia, were on the same subject. As prescribed, he handed in three tragedies and, as a lighter afterpiece, a satyr play. However, the three tragedies were on different themes. As a result, the drama itself had to be condensed and the frame of the action became narrower. The work of the poet became proportionately more difficult. To understand his task, we have only to keep in mind that it is more difficult to write a short novel than a long one. The internal plausibility of the plot easily suffers if the action has to be compressed, because all changes in the souls of the *dramatis personae* have to take place rapidly and yet must be sufficiently motivated.

According to Sophocles, the Oedipus legend runs as follows: Laius, king of Thebes, great-grandson of Cadmus, and his queen Jocasta were childless for a long time. Then after many years Jocasta gave birth to a boy. Since Laius had received an oracle from Apollo that the son born to him by Jocasta would slay his father and marry his mother, he ordered the boy to be exposed on Mount Cithaeron, with a spike driven through his feet. The servant charged with carrying out the order was moved by pity and placed the boy in the care of a Corinthian herdsman, who in turn brought him to his master, King Polybus. The king reared him as his son. After his swollen feet, the boy was called Oedipus ("the swollen-footed"). His putative parents left him in the dark concerning his descent, and when he was challenged on this question by companions at a banquet, he went to the oracle of Apollo at Delphi.

Here he was informed that it was his lot to slay his father and marry his mother. Alarmed, he did not return to Corinth but wandered toward Thebes. At a crossroad he met Laius, whom he did not know, and killed him in self-defense. At that time the highway leading to Thebes was harassed by the Sphinx, a monster with the face of a woman, the tail of a lion and the wings of a bird. To all passers-by the Sphinx presented its famous riddle: "What is it that is four-footed, three-footed, and two-footed?" Whoever failed to answer correctly was destroyed by the Sphinx who, on the other hand, had agreed to commit suicide in case anyone should answer correctly. The Thebans, anxious to have the highway cleared of the monster, had vowed that whoever was able to solve the riddle should be their next king. Oedipus gave the correct answer: "Man: for as a child he crawls on four feet, as an adult he walks on two, and as an old man he adds a cane."

Thereupon the Sphinx, fulfilling its part of the agreement, plunged to its death; Oedipus was hailed as the savior of Thebes and proclaimed king. He married Jocasta, the widow of Laius, by whom he had four children: Polynices and Eteocles, Antigone and Ismene. After many happy years a plague fell upon the city and the inhabitants turned to Oedipus for help.

It is at this point that Sophocles takes up the tale in his *Oedipus Rex,* the most famous of Greek dramas because no other is so filled with "tragic irony." The play opens with an impressive scene. A procession of suppliants, consisting of old men, youths and children, has come to the royal palace, carrying branches of laurel and olive wreathed with fillets of wool as symbols of supplication. They are seated on the steps of the altars in front of the palace and beseech Oedipus to offer appeasing sacrifices to the gods. The king tells them that, in his solicitude for the welfare of the city, he has sent his wife's brother, Creon, to Delphi to ask Apollo about the cause of the plague. At this moment Creon returns with the report that only the swift banishment or death of Laius's murderer will free the city, defiled by bloodshed, from the plague. Thereupon Oedipus calls down a bitter curse upon the murderer, whoever he may be, promising to leave nothing undone in order to apprehend him.

This opening scene has often been cited as a perfect example of the method advised by Horace in his *Ars Poetica* of plunging *in medias res,* that is, of beginning a narrative or a play not with what happened chronologically first but with some important event in "the midst of things," letting necessary explanations enter afterward. Sophocles could do this very easily: the connecting links were well known to his audience, since the story of Laius, Oedipus and the Sphinx was part of the folklore of the Greeks. The spectators knew therefore about the two oracles mentioned above—the one given to Laius, the other to his son Oedipus—that the son was to slay his father and marry his mother. It was a typical theme for Greek tragedy. A curse had been laid upon the royal house of Thebes because Laius had kidnaped the young son of Pelops and dishonored him. This sin caused a long chain of crimes ruining generation after generation.

Yet it is not the workings of an hereditary curse upon a family which forms the central theme of the Sophoclean tragedy. The oracle which Oedipus has received in reply to his inquiry concerning his descent is fulfilled at the beginning of the play, and he has lost every right of existence, according to the earlier oracle given to Laius. The poet has chosen rather the following theme: Oedipus, king of Thebes, is highly respected by his people as their savior from the vexation by the Sphinx and is altogether unaware that his own deeds, though committed unwillingly, have brought the plague upon the city. He takes upon himself the search for Laius's murderer who, according to the latest advice from Delphi, is still in the country. At the end this search leads to the dreadful realization—and nothing could be more tragic—that Oedipus himself is not only the slayer of his father but also the mate of his mother.

Thus the central theme of the drama is the self-identification of Oedipus, enacted step by step in exciting and most affecting scenes. First Oedipus asks the blind seer Tiresias to reveal the murderer. When the prophet declines to answer, the king sneers at his prophetic gift, thus compelling the seer to name Oedipus himself. Thereupon he suspects that Tiresias and Creon, the bearer of the latest oracle from Delphi, have plotted against him, and he threatens Creon with severe punishment.

In vain, Jocasta, in every respect the model of a faithful wife, tries to reassure her husband by pointing to the worthlessness of mantic art and even by explaining his rising suspicion as what some would today call a Freudian dream: "It has been the lot of many men in dreams to think themselves partners of their mother's bed; but who cares the least about these things lives the happiest." Oedipus reveals to Jocasta his past, including the oracle he has received in Delphi. The arrival of a messenger from Corinth, reporting the death of King Polybus, his putative father, gives him some comfort, but he is seized again with frightful anxiety when the messenger tells him that Oedipus had been committed to his care on Mount Cithaeron by a servant of King Laius. When this servant is called in and sees himself compelled to make a clean breast of what really took place, Oedipus gouges out his own eyes with the golden brooches of Jocasta who, seeing the identification complete, has hanged herself.

We may call *Oedipus Rex* an exciting novel in dramatic form, in which the judge and the person guilty of crime are one and the same. As a result, the whole stress is laid upon the action itself; characterization is only of secondary importance. Oedipus can hardly be characterized by his former deeds, committed without his knowing against whom he acted. Only one thing becomes clear from his prehistory—that in critical moments he has acted without sufficient circumspection and self-control, driven by the first impulse. It must be said, however, that these qualities, rashness and hot temper, also mark Oedipus' character in the tragedy. For instance, he rashly casts suspicion on Creon, who is well disposed toward him. His quick temper causes him to threaten with excessive punishment the old servant who tries to conceal the past in order to save his master. On the other hand, Oedipus possesses excellent qualities: an untiring devotion to his duties and a paternal solicitude for his people.

However, Oedipus wins our sympathy not so much by his character as by his dire fate, which has made him the man of sorrow in Greek mythology. And yet, only in part is *Oedipus Rex* a tragedy of Fate, because the poet presents his hero as master of his destiny, taking full responsibility for his deeds, whether done in ignorance or not. Thus it is chiefly from the character of Oedipus that Aristotle, in his *Poetics*, has derived his famous definition of the tragic hero, "a man who is highly renowned and prosperous, but one who is not preeminently virtuous and just, whose misfortune, however, is brought upon him not by vice and depravity but by some error of judgment or frailty." The tragic element is strengthened by the fate of Oedipus' loyal wife, Jocasta, who stands by the side of her son-husband from the very moment that quarrels have to be curbed and Oedipus himself consoled and reassured. For his sake, she even gives up her fear of the gods and her love of truth as long as she sees some remote chance to avert evil from the man she loves.

At the end of his life Sophocles returned once more to the Theban Saga to add a happy ending to the Oedipus story. This was in his *Oedipus at Colonus,* not included in the Great Books series, but here summarized to show the progress of the trilogy. Exiled from Thebes by Creon and his own sons, and accompanied by his loyal daughter Antigone, Oedipus wanders toward Athens. Exhausted by the long journey, he sits down in the shady grove of the Eumenides at Colonus, a suburb of Athens and Sophocles' native village. In vain Creon and, after him, Polynices try to induce the blind old man to return to Thebes. They are motivated by an oracle according to which Thebes would prosper only if Oedipus were interred in Theban land; if, however, he lay buried in Attica, Thebes would suffer and Athens prosper. Theseus, king of Athens, whom the poet pictures as an ideal ruler, gives him full protection. After having recommended his daughters to the latter, he sinks in a mysterious way to the gates of Hades. His grave is a seed of blessing for the land of Attica.

The central figure of this drama is a hero, purified by his sufferings, who has bravely renounced his useless fight against the gods. In picturing him, Sophocles attempted to solve as finally as possible for himself the problem which had occupied his mind all his life, how moral responsibility can be united to God's ways with man. To be sure, we do not find here the joyous resignation to God's will which we admire in the Christian martyrs. This notion was alien to antiquity. Yet the poet presents to us a hero not embittered and broken but exalted by his sufferings, who willingly gives himself up to the Erinyes or Furies, worshiped under the propitiatory name of Eumenides, or kindly powers, because he has finally understood and accepted his destiny, which is to be an instrument of that mysterious power governing the universe.

The third play of Sophocles' unintentional Theban trilogy carries the name of Antigone, Oedipus' loyal daughter, who had accompanied him into exile. After her father's death, she hurried back to Thebes in the hope of establishing peace between her two brothers, Polynices and Eteocles, who have quarreled about the Theban throne. But Polynices has been expelled from the country by Eteocles and has gone to Argos and married the daughter of King Adrastus. With a great host he has set out against Thebes to seize the throne. In a battle before the gates of Thebes the two brothers, meeting in individual combat, fall by each other's hand, thus fulfilling the curse their father had called upon them just before his death. Thereupon, Creon, now king of Thebes, issues an order that full funeral honors be given to the body of Eteocles while the corpse of Polynices, a traitor to his native land, should lie unburied. At this point the play opens.

Antigone, who values piety and the love of her brother and who regards divine law above man-made decrees, defies Creon's order and buries her brother after her timid sister Ismene has refused to assist her. Caught while performing the burial rites, she is condemned to be buried alive in spite of the intercession of Ismene and Haemon, Creon's son and Antigone's bridegroom. She hangs herself in her sepulchral chamber, a rock-tomb in the low hills which fringe the plain of Thebes. She is found by Haemon, who is now resolved to die. Threatened by the seer Tiresias with impending disaster, Creon decides to free Antigone. But it is too late. Haemon stabs himself, and his mother Eurydice likewise dies by her own hand.

The central theme of the drama is the conflict arising from the moral conviction of the heroine that the eternal, unwritten laws should take precedence over human ordinances. Though the heroine and two members of her family fall victims to a horrible fate, man-made law bows at the end before the divine. Creon is punished for his insolence. The moral of the play is contained in the closing words of the drama: "Wisdom is the supreme part of happiness; and reverence toward the gods must be inviolate. Great words of overproud men bring great punishments and in old age teach the chastened to be wise."

RUDOLPH ARBESMANN

SELECTED BIBLIOGRAPHY

BOWRA, C. M., *Sophoclean Tragedy*. Oxford (The Clarendon Press).
HAMILTON, E., *The Greek Way*. Norton.
SHEPPARD, J. T., *Aeschylus and Sophocles, Their Work and Influence*. Longmans, Green.
SHOREY, P., *Sophocles* (Martin Classical Lectures, Vol. I). Harvard University.
WEBSTER, T. B. L., *An Introduction to Sophocles*. Oxford (The Clarendon Press).
SOPHOCLES, *Dramas*. Dutton (Everyman's Library).
SOPHOCLES, *Oedipus the King, Antigone*. Regnery.

Aristotle: The Poetics

THE CONTINUED VITALITY of Aristotle's tantalizingly brief and deceptively simple treatise, *The Poetics* (composed between 335 and 322 B.C.), hardly needs demonstration. Mention of Lane Cooper's *The Poetics of Aristotle, Its Meaning and Influence,* Cooper and Gudeman's *A Bibliography of The Poetics of Aristotle,* or Marvin T. Herrick's *The Poetics of Aristotle in England* serves to recall how Aristotle's ideas have influenced virtually all critics in the Western community of nations up to the twentieth century. This influence was transmitted by direct translation and paraphrase, by adaptation and selective quotation. Frequently Aristotle's enormous prestige was borrowed to lend authority to dogmas which Aristotle himself would probably disown. But, more or less accurately, Aristotle's views on poetry have survived the centuries. His concept of art as imitation, his theory of catharsis in tragedy, his insistence on the necessary unity and variety of plot, his description of the virtues of the ideal tragic hero, his distinction between tragedy and comedy, and between various kinds of plot—all these have formed our common thinking not only about dramatic and epic poetry, with which his treatise is primarily concerned, but about literature and the fine arts in general.

The Aristotelian yeast is in Horace (by way of Neoptolemus of Parium) and Dante, in Minturno and Castelvetro, in Sidney and Ben Jonson, in Milton and Dryden, in Corneille and Boileau, in Johnson and Pope, in Coleridge and Newman, in Churton Collins and John Crowe Ransom, in T. S. Eliot and Maxwell Anderson. Some of these critics and writers have gone to *The Poetics* to find a rational defense for poetry, others to explore its technical insights, a few to recapture the intellectual experience of a critic who contemplated literature with the discriminating love of the philosopher, the accuracy of the grammarian, the pathetic instincts of the rhetorician, the concrete realistic sense of the historian: of a critic, in short, who brought to bear on the origin, purpose and technique of literary expression the full powers of a great mind.

Now, the problems to which Aristotle addressed himself in *The Poetics* were basically of two kinds: one was a problem of the origin and end of poetry; the other a problem of means. The first problem involves the question of how poetry originated and what is its purpose in the lives of men who are at once individuals and citizens of a community. The second problem involves the technical artistic questions of how the best artists use the best means to achieve the appropriate poetic end. In solving the basic questions of ends and means Aristotle answered, *pari passu,* the five objections commonly urged against the poets of his day by severe moralists and literal grammarians—charges which, as he stated them in Chapter XXV—could be summed up under the headings of absurdity, irrationality, immorality, inconsistency and bad technique.

The discussion of the origin and purpose of poetry, which is inconveniently scattered throughout his treatise, was not provoked by the philosopher's isolated curiosity alone. The question had been a burning one in fourth-century Athens. Plato, Aristotle's master, had once, in his *Ion* and *Phaedrus,* explained poetry as a kind of divine madness, a benign daemonic possession. But, as Plato became more and more concerned with the laws governing the well-ordered state and more confirmed in his much-debated theories on the origin of ideas and the nature of truth, his dialogs discharged increasingly heavy criticism against poetry and poets. In Book II of *The Republic,* Plato in the character of Socrates contended that the poets mislead the young and the uneducated by telling lies about the gods, presenting them as vain, angry and lustful, whereas God in truth is all perfect. Famous heroes were likewise said to be misrepresented in a welter of unseemly tears and incontinent laughter. Socrates enters a strong plea for licensing only those poets who imitate pure virtue, a sentiment which Plato repeated in Book II of *The Laws.*

In Book X of *The Republic* Socrates returned to his attack on the poets from the point of view of imitation. Despite his veneration for Homer, Socrates says: "All the imitative arts seem to me ruinous to the mental powers of all their hearers who do not

have as an antidote the knowledge of what these arts really are."
What these arts really are, he infers, is not direct contact with
truth, but an imitation of the outward appearances of reality, the
imitation of an imitation, and are therefore at least thrice removed from truth. The poet, then, imitates "without knowing
how each thing is good or bad, but what seems excellent to the
ignorant rabble . . . he knows nothing worth mentioning of
what he imitates, but his imitation is a sort of game and not
serious. . . . Can there be any doubt that this imitation is not
in direct contact with truth?" No trivial error, this corrupting
delight of poetry. It fed and nurtured the sexual emotions, anger
and all the passions, sorrows and pleasures of the spirit, which a
prudent man should strive to dry up. Poetry put passions in command "when they should be so ruled that we may grow better
and happier instead of worse and more vile." Small wonder then
that Socrates finally condemns the poets to be banished from the
ideal state.

Thus, at the very outset, Aristotle encountered the opposition
of Plato in an objection which, formidable in itself, was rendered
even more plausible by Plato's extensive knowledge and love of
poetry as well as by his magnificent style.

How did Aristotle answer this objection? He had explicitly
denied Plato's theory of ideas, in *The Metaphysics* and elsewhere
in his philosophical works. But in *The Poetics* he merely advanced another idea of imitation which implicitly contradicted
the idea of imitation held by Plato. All art, Aristotle agreed, was
imitation. The various arts were distinguished from each other
and among themselves by the medium, objects and manner of
imitation (Chapter I). The object of artistic imitation was men
in action; some of these actions were good, some bad, some indifferent (Chapter II). Aristotle here merely states a fact of history. The good, bad and indifferent characters, men as they are,
as they were said to be and as they should be, had been objects
of imitation in the evolution of Greek painting, poetry and music,
and fine art in general.

When he turns to literature to distinguish beween the drama
and narrative poetry, and between tragedy and comedy, Aristotle
allows this history to dispute Plato's theory of imitation. "Speaking generally," he writes in Chapter IV, "poetry seems to owe its
origin to two particular causes, both natural." First it is man's

nature to know by imitation; secondly he derives great pleasure by and from imitation. Men who are not philosophers derive virtually all the necessary human pleasures of contemplation by reasoning and pondering upon actions presented in works of art, whether these actions bear the exalted character of tragedy or the pedestrian character of comedy.

Such pleasure, Aristotle argues, is not folly. It is in accordance with men's nature. Neither is poetic imitation—the cause of this pleasure—the folly or ignorance imputed to it by Plato. For poetic imitation is an entirely different kind of knowledge from that according to which Plato had measured poetry and found it wanting. The poet, says Aristotle in Chapter IX, is not an historian dealing with actual events and bound by particular facts; neither is he a philosopher who uses concrete particulars as a starting point for his primary business of abstraction. The poet is concerned rather with the general or idealized truth inseparable from concrete human action. Hence poetry is more serious and philosophic than history, a term for which modern readers find a rough equivalent in De Quincey's "literature of knowledge." Whereas history deals with parts unified by chronological sequence, poetry deals with a whole action with its own beginning, middle and end, and is governed by the law of intrinsic probability or necessity.

Furthermore, since poetry is an imitation of human action, the poet is not obliged to present only virtuous action. He is justified in representing men not only as they should be but as they are, as they are said to be; and, in comedy at least, as worse than they are, so long as he does not deceive himself or his audience as to the right moral attitude. The poet will not be deceitful, Aristotle implies, if the circumstances of the whole action and the particular speeches are examined as carefully as testimony submitted to a jury or the proofs offered in debate (Chapter XXV). What Aristotle suggests then is that the presentation of immoral actions is not in itself immoral when such actions are rightly seen as unlawful in deed and tragic in outcome.

Plato's objection to poetry on the grounds that it was thrice removed from reality was thus explained by another theory of imitation. By showing that the *raison d'être* of all art is placed in the pleasure of imitation, in "man's intrinsic desire to know all things on the level of imagination rather than on the higher and for most men impossible level of speculation" (Mortimer Adler), Aristotle rescued men from a false dilemma presented in the compulsory choice between truth without art or art without truth.

Moreover, Aristotle blunted Plato's moralistic censure in the same argument. If the object of poetry was the contemplative pleasure of imitation and not the direct imitation of abstract truth, then it could not be held responsible for the explicit performance of a moral office. Its good moral effect could come by indirect means. Poetry could rest and re-create the mind of its audience; dispose that mind to higher contemplation; cleanse it of folly; purge it of the painful emotions of pity and fear. Art performed its public duty by providing that rational entertainment, the pleasure of knowing through imitation, without which men would be a prey to animal appetites and passions.

Imitation thus rendered pleasurable in art what was painful in life. But what was painful in art, the emotions of pity and fear proper to tragedy, was also rendered pleasurable, according to Aristotle, by the theory of catharsis. This much-disputed term, for which Bywater found sixty variant translations, has never been satisfactorily explained. That a catharsis takes place we know by reference to the familiar Sophoclean and Shakespearean touchstones. How it takes place, what psychological processes it involves, is the source of continuing speculation.

The earliest modern commentator on *The Poetics*, Casalio (1520), suggested that a good tragic writer succeeded in purging painful emotions by forewarning the spectator of actual grief, by regulating the exercise of pity and fear and finally by reconciling the spectator to misfortune and the tragic sense of life. Each succeeding age interpreted the cathartic principle according to its own lights. Most writers have followed the medical implications of the word catharsis. A "homeopathic" school felt that to witness fictitious pain might lessen real suffering. The "pathologists" (Milton subscribed to this view) argue that the tragic catharsis moderated a disturbing "humor." It has been decided that compassion and terror purged the mind, calmed agitated nervous systems (I. A. Richards), corrected ethical bias, adjusted emotions to reality. An esthetic school maintains that tragedy permits the spectator to release potentially aggressive energies in the comparative safety of a spiritual gymnasium.

But if catharsis defies complete description, it is nevertheless as recognizable in its effects as the equally mysterious literary power which Longinus called the sublime. We are as grateful for the hint as we are impatient for a final solution.

II

However, the bulk of Aristotle's *The Poetics* is concerned not with the origin and end of art but with its formal organization, the means by which art achieves its end, the laws, empirically determined, which shape the actions of men to a kind of beauty by the right ordering of separate incidents. It is in this area of criticism that Aristotle's genius for subtle analysis is displayed with compelling force.

First he defined the principal genres of poetry: comedy, an imitation of characters of a lower class than tragedy, was the representation of a painless incongruity; the epic, an imitation of characters of a higher type, was similar to tragedy except that it was narrative rather than dramatic and required a less exacting unity of action. Aristotle's treatment of comedy is also scanty, and he employed the epic as a topic of comparison with tragedy rather than as a subject for separate and searching examination. He concentrated on tragedy, no doubt because the tragedies of his day offered the best samples of true art and because the most artistic elements in other forms of poetry were also visible in the tragic context.

"Tragedy, then," says Aristotle in Professor Butcher's translation, "is an imitation of an action that is serious, complete [with a beginning, middle and end] and of a certain magnitude [long enough to sustain an illusion of reality, not so long as to be confusing]; in language embellished with each kind of artistic ornament . . . in the form of action, not of narrative; through pity and fear effecting the proper purgation of these emotions." Every tragedy was composed of six parts; plot, character, diction, thought, spectacle and song, the most important of which was plot.

Aristotle's emphasis on plot, which he calls the soul of a tragedy, is particularly significant. To him plot was not merely a mechanical device by means of which the chief characters were trapped in the meshes of a preordained fate; nor was it merely a well-made sequence of events. Plot was rather a life force, an animat-

ing principle of selection, the grasp of the total meaning of a
series of incidents, a rendering of a particular action in such a
way as to reveal its relation to life as a whole. Plot caught thought
emerging like Aphrodite from the foam of fact. Plot shaped incidents into recognizable unity not by assembling the parts but by
fusing the elements. An episode, however real, might not contribute to the plot; dialog, however natural and consistent, con-
ceivably could distract from the organic unity of the basic incidents. The most effective spectacle or theatrical presentation, or
the most exalted lyric music also must draw its life and significance from plot. Even character, which is the central considera-
tion in most modern dramatists, was subordinated to plot because,
as Aristotle points out, it is possible to see a meaningful pattern
in events without characterization.

Yet Aristotle managed to stress plot without minimizing the
importance of the other elements. On the contrary, the primacy
of plot tended to protect the rightful place of character, thought,
diction, spectacle and song in the artistic hierarchy. The tragic
character, for example, is more clearly defined and his importance
preserved under the government of plot.

The proper tragic hero, says Aristotle, is natural, consistent
and universal or representative. His significance in speech or act
is consequent upon a moral choice. He is what he is in terms of
his deliberate reactions to events of which he is a part. As far as
drama is concerned, he has no existence except within the frame-
work of plot. If he speaks or acts outside this frame of reference
he is merely an unnecessary bystander. The government of plot,
of the reality in the appearances—an inference drawn, it cannot
be too often repeated, from the practice of the best tragic writers
of the Athenian stage—also accounts for Aristotle's insistence
that the true tragic hero is essentially a good man with a damag-
ing flaw in his character. For if the tragic hero were an eminently
good and faultless man, we would be shocked by the outcome of
the plot; or if, on the other hand, he were a villain, we would
be bound to applaud his defeat rather than to sympathize with
his suffering.

Similarly the control of the whole tragic synthesis by plot in-
sures the fruitful employment of thought, the reasonings and
conclusions of the actors and the chorus, and the lyric element of
song. If these elements were present for their own sake they

would violate the artistic economy which Aristotle stated with his usual succinctness thus: "For a thing whose presence or absence makes no visible difference [in the structural union of the parts] is not an organic part of the whole." Without plot a drama would be a series of recitations delivered in costume, a string of episodes, a vaudeville pretending to be art.

Plot is not mere device in *The Poetics;* but device has its place too. Device is the employment of tactic under the strategy of plot; it is secondary, instrumental but necessary. Not the least rewarding sections of the treatise deal with the technical problems of plot device. In Chapter XIII Aristotle mentions the simple and complex plot and debates whether it is better to trace the reversal from bad fortune to good fortune as well as from good fortune to bad in the same play. He finds (Chapter XIV) the most terrible and pitiable actions to be those which result from the inner structure of the fiction—deeds of horror done among friends through ignorance or mistake. Recognition, the chief instrument for effecting tragic irony (whose modern equivalent is the term "suspense"), explains how the gradually intensified and terrifying discovery of the tragic predicament yields far more astonishment than bare surprise (Chapter XVI). A definition of complication and resolution or dénouement; a division of tragedy into four kinds, the complex, the pathetic, the ethical and the simple, and a comparison with the epic conclude Aristotle's discussion of structure in the drama (Chapter XVIII).

That Aristotle was partly a practical as well as a theoretic critic, concerned not merely with the place of poetry in the economy of knowledge, but also with immediate questions of artistic prudence, will be readily recognized from the foregoing remarks on plot. But he is not, in our own times, sufficiently credited for his practical judgments. The "New Criticism" of I. A. Richards, William Empson, John Crowe Ransom and Cleanth Brooks is somewhat less emancipated from Aristotle than its revolutionary pretensions would allow one to suppose. The new critics' stress on metaphor finds an Aristotelian precedent in Aristotle's statement that "the right use of metaphor is a sign of genius"; their discovery of ambiguity is anticipated by Aristotle's defense in Chapter XXV of *The Poetics* of the same practice by Homer— with the words "the explanation is that of ambiguity."

Similarly the necessity of reading a poem in its context was foreshadowed when Aristotle wrote that "things that sound contradictory should be examined by the rules of dialectic—whether the same thing is meant, in the same relation, and in the same sense." The busy contemporary word "tone," generally understood to mean the attitude a writer assumes toward his material and his audience, might well be used as a free translation for the Aristotelian idea that meaning is sometimes determined by reference to what may be tacitly assumed in a person of intelligence. The contemporary critical concentration on paradox has an Aristotelian parallel in Chapter XXII. Here Aristotle declares that the perfection of style consists in being clear without being mean. He sanctions what he calls "a certain infusion" of strange, riddling, metaphorical words with proper perspicuous words and grants the poetic license to deviate from the normal idiom to achieve distinction. It may not be extravagant to say that Chapter XXII also deals with the general problem of the "conceit." Certainly Aristotle had a metaphysical point in mind when he praised the command of metaphor as a sure sign that the writer could see and express the hidden resemblances of objects. But he was not so "metaphysical" in our sense of the term that he did not demand moderation, propriety, an art which concealed art.

Still another kind of practicality may be observed in *The Poetics* in the series of Horatian literary expediencies, sometimes delivered as informal asides, sometimes connected with the basic argument. The poet is warned about the employment of signs or tokens of recognition. He is advised to speak in his own person as little as possible and urged to visualize his plot as though he were a spectator of the action. Diction too splendid is liable to conceal both character and thought, Aristotle tells the poet. Critics and audiences come to expect more of later dramatists than they do of their predecessors, so that the writer is enjoined to include all types of appeal in his dramas. Violent action should take place off stage. Accidental violations of historical truth do not destroy the essential truth of poetry. Beauty consists of magnitude and order and thus a play must have a proper beginning, middle and end. The episodic plots are the worst of all. No complication should be solved by the *deus ex machina*. The chorus should be regarded as one of the actors. Aristotle missed few of the "how to write" truisms, just as he missed few of the major critical problems.

These many sides of *The Poetics*—and there are several more which lack of space forbids us to display—simply reveal the totality of view with which Aristotle analyzed the question of imaginative literature. He saw poetry as a whole and in its parts, its appeal to eye through spectacle, to the ear through music and diction, to the reason through thought, to all the faculties of sense, intellect and intuition through the synthesis of plot. He saw too the limitations of criticism, how bad critics find the poets guilty of disobeying laws decreed by the critics' own improper authority. Far from banishing mystery from the creation of a work of art, Aristotle regarded poetic genius as a happy gift of nature or a power of ecstasy (Chapter XVII), akin to Plato's divine enthusiasm.

In seeing all this, he has helped subsequent generations immeasurably in the common human effort to realize our common human predicament by way of art, in which joy sings and sorrow suffers a sea change into something rich, strange and beautiful.

FRANCIS X. CONNOLLY

SELECTED BIBLIOGRAPHY

ADLER, M., *Art and Prudence.* Longmans, Green.
ATKINS, J. W. H., *Literary Criticism in Antiquity, Vol. I.* Cambridge.
BUTCHER, S. H., *Aristotle's Theory of Poetry and Fine Art.* Macmillan.
BYWATER, I., *Aristotle on the Art of Poetry.* Oxford.
COOPER, L., *The Poetics of Aristotle.* Longmans, Green.
GILBERT, A. H., *Aristotle's The Poetics in Literary Criticism.* American Book.
ROSS, W. D., *Aristotle.* Oxford.
ARISTOTLE, *The Poetics.* Dutton (Everyman's Library).
ARISTOTLE, *Poetics.* Regnery.
COOPER, L., and GUDEMAN, A., *A Bibliography of The Poetics of Aristotle.* Cornell University Press.
HERRICK, M. T., *The Poetics of Aristotle in England.* Cornell University Press.

Plato: *Meno*

THE DIALOG *Meno* has a unique place in the Platonic canon. It marks Plato's breaking through to his greatest discovery, that there is a type of knowledge which is absolute in character and which is realized by the human mind within itself: the cognition of essence. With this not only does Plato come into his own, but in a way so does the whole of Western philosophy.

To state that *Meno* contains Plato's first version of his most famous doctrine, the Doctrine of Ideas, is certainly true, but it places the emphasis on that which is only of secondary importance. The Doctrine of Ideas is only Plato's attempt to cope theoretically with his discovery, to interpret it and to explain it. The importance of the discovery of cognition of essence, however, greatly outstrips the value of a mere interpretation. The Platonic Doctrine of Ideas, with its implications, with the difficult problems into which it leads, with its grandeur and limitations, is an historical reality of the first magnitude.

Plato's discovery, however, is more than that: like any great discovery, it is a common possession of mankind. It belongs to the awakened and articulate condition of human existence which we call "civilization." To forsake this discovery would be a part of a process of rebarbarization. In this very profound sense it belongs to our heritage, as poetry does or the art of government by popular consent, and not as Homer's epics or the Magna Carta. Certainly Plato's Doctrine of Ideas, just as Homer's epics, could not be left out of any true picture of Western civilization. It has proved so thought-provoking that one has called the whole of the history of Western philosophy "footnotes on Plato." But with Plato's discovery there is a difference: it is a part of ourselves.

Wherever philosophers do their work, they strive for the knowledge of essence. They do what Plato brought to articulate awareness for the first time—what he discovered, not what he invented. He and others, especially Socrates, had done it before Plato focused his mind upon it for the first time. And philosophers are exercising the art of "essence cognition" whether or not they are disposed to render tribute to the fact and to the man who first brought it to the light of consciousness.

To an amazing degree philosophers underestimate the impact of the Platonic discovery. The numerous quarrels about the interpretations of the fact have unhappily overshadowed the importance of the fact. Overconcerned with one specific version about philosophic cognition, philosophers too often overlook the truth that to philosophize means, in spite of all special theories, exactly what Plato had pointed at, what he brought to light and attempted to describe. His description is imperfect, but the thing described is there, and *Meno* is the moment in Plato's development where the *"prise de conscience"* of philosophic cognition takes place. This is the ultimate greatness of *Meno* and it is this which indisputably places that Platonic dialog in the ranks of the Great Books of mankind.

The setting of the dialog is one of unusual simplicity. It is for the most part a direct conversation between Meno, a young Thessalian, and Socrates. With striking abruptness it begins with Meno's asking: "Can you tell me, Socrates, if virtue can be taught?" Later on, at a dramatic turn of the conversation, a young, uneducated slave boy is called and questioned by Socrates as an experiment to demonstrate his point. This experiment is the climax of the dialog. The first part leads up to it, and its results are evaluated in the latter part, where for a brief time, in a kind of gloomy interlude, Anytus makes his appearance.

Meno in all probability was written toward the end of the first period of Plato's activities, those ten or twelve years between the death of Socrates (399 B.C.) and the founding of the Academy. It is believed to have followed the publication of *Protagoras* and *Gorgias* and may very well be the last of Plato's earlier writings.

Meno takes up *the* Socratic problem—"what is virtue?"—where the earlier writings had left it. In the so-called minor Socratic dialogs (such as *Charmides* or *Laches*) a number of virtues— temperance, courage, etc.—had been examined. Consistently the discussion is left without any final result, the participants failing to agree upon a "definition" of the virtue in question. But two things are emphasized throughout: first, that specific virtues are "parts" of virtue itself and therefore can be understood only after an understanding of virtue itself has been achieved; second, that virtue is essentially a kind of "knowledge," of good sense and understanding (*sophrosyne*), of, we may venture to say, "value awareness."

If it is a kind of knowledge, then it must be teachable—that is the theme of the dialog *Protagoras*. If it is teachable, then it must be taught to the politicians, who are most desperately in need of virtue if they are to run the affairs of the city justly and beneficially—such as the leading idea of *Gorgias*.

The direct question with which *Meno* opens connects the dialog with its forerunners. Socrates refuses to answer the question of whether virtue is teachable before the other question, "what is virtue?", is answered. Meno's futile attempts to reply by employing the sophistic style of his teacher Gorgias give ample occasion for a marvelous display of the Socratic technique of refutation. The negating part of the Socratic method is shown here with unsurpassed mastery.

Meno, instead of answering the question what virtue is, begins by describing the various forms it takes with people differing in age or sex or social condition. After such a procedure is rejected by Socrates, Meno begins to talk about this and that specific virtue, producing "a swarm of virtues" instead of virtue itself. His attempt to define virtue with the help of one of the virtues involves him in a vicious circle. Socrates shows the futility of this attempt: "You should not suppose that while the nature of virtue as a whole is still under inquiry you could explain it to anyone by replying in terms of its parts, or by any other statement along the same lines: you will only have to face the same question over again" (79 DE).

The dramatic turn comes when Meno finally realizes what Socrates has in mind but makes this objection: "In what direction will you look, Socrates, for a thing about whose nature you know nothing at all? What sort of thing, among those things about which you do not know, can you present to us as the object of your search? Or even supposing, at the best, that you did find what you were looking for, how will you know it is the thing you did not know?" (8 OD).

Socrates acknowledges the seriousness of such an objection: somebody who knows does not need to inquire, somebody who does not know cannot inquire, and thus all searching would be stopped.

Up to this point Plato has depicted Socrates in his characteristic manner, true to the literary picture which had been given in earlier dialogs. Socrates could have handled the discussion in the way it is here presented, although it might be doubted that he had the degree of logical refinement which Plato exhibits in this dialog.

But now Socrates is at a point of deep perplexity. It is unlike the perplexity of other dialogs, where Socrates confesses to be at a loss as far as a positive solution of this or that problem is concerned. Here the whole Socratic undertaking is in jeopardy. This problem cannot be left unsolved, and Plato has conceived a solution. But to put it simply in the mouth of Socrates would be untrue to the literary picture of his revered teacher. With the sovereign mastery of the accomplished writer, Plato uses a device which enables him to remain true to the character of Socrates and yet to say what he has to say.

Here for the first time (with the possible exception of the myth at the end of *Gorgias*) Plato speaks completely for himself and makes it clear that he does so. Socrates gives the solution of the problem of how searching is possible at all, by relating something he has heard from "priests and priestesses" and from "poets of heavenly gifts" (81 A), and though he is not sure whether it is true as it stands, he accepts it gladly, because it enables him to continue the searching which is the very purport of his life. What is this solution?

The divines have told Socrates that the soul is immortal, having had a preexistence "where she has learned of all things without exception, so that it is no wonder that she should be able to remember what virtue and all other things are" (81 C). Knowledge, therefore, is recollection. In searching our memory, we do not know the thing we seek, but the moment we hit upon it, we suddenly do know that this is the thing we were looking for. The same is true in the searching we call philosophy. Thus, to understand philosophically seems to be a kind of recollection.

The Plato who speaks in this "myth" and meets the Plato who is the disciple of Socrates, is the heir of Pythagoras, Plato the metaphysician with the deeply religious mind who feels the vocation to enlighten his belief by a sober intellectual searching:

"Those who say so are priests and priestesses, who have studied how they might be able to give a reason to their profession" (81 AB).

This remark is of the utmost importance. Plato's problem is not only: how can our absolute knowledge (e.g., our moral knowledge) be explained, since it is not explainable by our sense contact with the world about us? His problem is also: how can the religious belief in immortality, in preexistence, in something divine, high above us and yet as real as we are ourselves—how can the belief in all this be supported by any observable fact and thus be made reasonable?

Certainly, Socrates' method of searching needed some metaphysical foundation, such as Socrates himself had never furnished. But also the ancient belief in another world was in need of some empirical support, by the discovery of some trace of the absolute within the world of our common experience. And here it is discovered: the fact of absolute knowledge is a proof of the preexistence (and even the full immortality) of the soul and of the substantiality of a higher world: "Now if the truth of all things that are, is always in our soul, then the soul must be immortal" (86 A). The belief meets the experience and is upheld by it as the experience is explained by the belief. From now on Plato begins to be able "to give a reason for his profession."

This certainly was a great moment in Plato's development. Suddenly the separated realms in his mind fused. The implications of his recollection metaphysics, of the doctrine of "existing" ideas had not yet been envisioned, and their heavy weight had not yet been felt. It must have been a moment of intense intellectual delight when Plato discovered that this longing for a higher world of absolute reality and his disciplined logical searching were not two incompatible trends of his mind, but mutually supported one another.

From the "myth" Plato turns to the experiment. Meno's skeptical question has found an answer which comes to this: we can acquire knowledge of what we did not know, if knowledge, like recollections, is an inner recognizing of what we had as knowledge in us, but had forgotten. The experiment is to show that knowledge indeed does have this character.

An uneducated slave boy is asked to perform a task of geometry. He is only questioned, never "instructed." The boy makes all the naïve mistakes of someone not versed in the field. But when his errors are shown to him, he "sees" them until he finally comes to the right solution and realizes its inner necessity. It is this point which Plato wants to make clear: there is a grasping of the inner necessity of things, a grasping of what cannot be different. The kind of knowledge under inquiry seeks to come to an inner evidence about objects of absolute necessity. Once grasped, this evidence results in conviction. The process leads to "exact understanding." Such understanding cannot be transmitted from the outside. Teaching in such a case can only consist in helping what has to be performed within the mind. That such a kind of knowledge exists, the experiment is to demonstrate.

Plato uses the mathematical example—although he later (in *The Republic*) works out the difference between this realm and the realm of moral knowledge—because in mathematics the kind of knowledge he has in mind presents itself in its purest form. But the implication is that the knowledge of the Good is, in principle, of the same kind. Mathematics is the best proving ground for the establishment of knowledge which is unempirical, because it is so clearly beyond that which can be grasped by the senses, and so undeniably true knowledge. The depth and complexity of the moral sphere would soon lead to a dispute in which the transempirical and objective character of this whole kind of knowledge could easily become obscured and so the very fact of such a kind of knowledge be doubted.

Socrates restricts himself to the acceptance of the fact of transempirical knowledge. He does not take a definite stand in favor of the explanation which the myth affords for the results of the experiment. He is restricting himself to the pragmatic position that the meaningfulness of searching has been proved and that a deeper interpretation of the Socratic method of leading a conversation into perplexities is discernible. He says of the boy: "Do you imagine he would have attempted to inquire or learn what he thought he knew, when he did not know it, until he has been reduced to the perplexity of realizing that he did not know, and had felt a craving to know?" (84 C).

And so, confirmed in his ways, he immediately sets out anew with the old question: what is virtue? On the insistence of Meno, however, he agrees to concentrate for the time being on the secondary question: is virtue teachable? The taking up of that second point is possible only if one agrees on some "hypothetical" solution of the question: what is virtue? The hypothesis offered is that virtue is "of the soul"—is something mental and something similar to knowledge. If, and only if, it is a kind of knowledge, of right understanding (*sophrosyne*), is it teachable. But is it a kind of knowledge? This is answered affirmatively by the argument that it is always the presence of *sophrosyne* which makes an otherwise ambiguous behavior good. Courage, for example, minus prudence would be nothing but boldness, and so similarly with other virtues. This permits the conclusion that virtue is either wholly or partly a kind of knowledge, and so the hypothetical condition is fulfilled and therefore the assumption seems to be justified that virtue is teachable.

The dialog might have ended here, with the positive result that virtue is teachable. But Plato throws everything into the open again by having Socrates revert to his skeptical mood. Plato had expressed an unbounded optimism when he presented the myth by saying: "If the truth of all things that are, is always in our soul, then the soul must be immortal; so that you should take heart, and whatever you do not happen to know at present— that is, what you do not remember—you must endeavor to search out and recollect" (86 AB). But he does not want to convey the impression that this is easily done. "Plato pushed impetuously on toward knowledge. And yet he took Socrates' ignorance to be a sign of his true greatness, for he thought it was the birth pangs of a new kind of knowledge struggling to be born of Socrates' travailing mind."

So, in true Socratic style the result just established is questioned again. How can it be that virtue is teachable where we do not find teachers of virtue? The Sophists have to be disregarded. That they are even mentioned provokes the violent reaction of Anytus, and we understand how he could in the narrowness of his mind accuse Socrates of the very thing against which he was fighting like no one else, the Sophistic misleading of youth.

Since virtue actually is not taught, and since it cannot be denied that there were virtuous men among the great figures of Athenian political life, such as Themistocles and Aristides, then there must be a way of becoming virtuous other than by being taught. Such a way may be divine dispensation. But to decide about such a solution would necessitate a return to the question: what is virtue? Thus the dialog, like all its predecessors, ends with an open question.

But the result is only seemingly negative. For, if the closing part demonstrates that virtue is not taught in the conventional meaning of the term, it makes much more strongly felt the necessity of applying the findings of the middle part of the dialog to the whole question. Virtue, understood as a kind of knowledge which can be grasped only within one's own mind, but which cannot be transmitted by informative teaching, needs a new kind of "teacher," one who is capable of helping souls to free themselves so that they may make all the great discoveries within themselves. It needs "the philosopher" as he is described in the greatest of all Platonic writings, *The Republic.*

So *Meno* leads beyond itself. It points forward in the direction of greater things to come. But it has established the confidence in that ethos of unwavering intellectual searching for which Socrates was the inspiring example for Plato. And so it may be fitting to finish these remarks with a quotation in which the Socrates of the dialog *Meno* summarizes his intellectual and moral position: "Most of the points I have made in support of my argument are not such as I can confidently assert; but that the belief in the duty of inquiring after what we do not know will make us better and braver and less helpless than the notion that there is not even a possibility of discovering what we do not know, nor any duty of inquiring after it—this is a point for which I am determined to do battle, so far as I am able, both in word and deed" (86 BC).

BALDUIN V. SCHWARZ

SELECTED BIBLIOGRAPHY

LAMB, W. R. M., *Plato, With an English Translation.* Putnam (Loeb Classical Library).

JOWETT, B., *The Dialogues of Plato, Translated into English with Analyses and Introduction.* Scribner.

TAYLOR, A. E., *Plato, the Man and His Work.* Dial.

STENZEL, Julius, *Plato's Method of Dialectic.* Oxford (The Clarendon Press).

JAEGER, Werner, *Paideia: The Ideals of Greek Culture.* Oxford.

PLATO, *Dialogues* (2 vols.). Dutton (Everyman's Library).

PLATO, *The Meno.* Regnery.

7

Aristotle: Ethics, *Books II, IV and VI*

IN THE BEGINNING of the second book of the *Nicomachean Ethics,*
Aristotle starts with the fundamental distinction between moral
virtues and intellectual perfections. He sees the difference between moral and intellectual values, a distinction which is indispensable to an understanding of the unique character and position of moral virtues. He stresses the fact that, whereas intellectual perfections are acquired by being taught, moral virtues are
attained by practice, by one's becoming accustomed to act in
conformity with morality. This Aristotelian thesis, which has had
so great an influence, is a typical example of how genuine discoveries and abstract constructions are in some peculiar way intermingled in the theories of many a great philosopher.

Aristotle saw that moral virtue implies an "easy acting" in
conformity with morality. This is a deep insight which Kant, for
instance, completely overlooked in his ethics. Aristotle rightly
saw also that the attaining of a moral virtue requires a *repeated*
acting in conformity with morality. But he confuses this function
of a repeated morally good acting with the role which custom
and practice play in other fields of human life, such as in the
biological sphere, in some of the arts and in the learning of
languages. We acquire certain biological tendencies by becoming
accustomed to certain things. We learn a poem by often repeating
the verses. We attain skill in playing an instrument by practicing.

But this power of habit and practice has a completely technical
character and operates through channels which are below the
spiritual level of man in the proper sense. The acquisition of
moral virtues, on the contrary, necessarily implies the cooperation of our specifically spiritual faculties. It is never the merely
technical automatism of custom that endows us with moral virtues. In reality there are many more factors in the process. Among
them are the knowledge of the morally good, the depth of the

will responding to the morally good, the spiritual knowledge we choose, recollection, the moral climate in which we live, the influence of moral authority and our obedience to it, and last but not least all kinds of asceticism performed to surmount the obstacles in our nature.

But even in what concerns the role of a repeated good acting we have to grasp the fact that this implies, first, the fully conscious and free response to values and, second, that it has the character of a victorious penetration of our entire personality by the conscious and free value response, a becoming rooted in the realm of morality rather than being the mere technical repetition which leads us to skill in extramoral spheres. The mere automatism of custom, in the properly spiritual sphere and especially in the moral sphere, is on the contrary rather a danger, which tends to replace virtues by a mere routine. It is very characteristic of Aristotle's procedure in the whole of the *Nicomachean Ethics* that in Book VI he corrects to a great extent this reduction to habit, as we shall see later on.

The main content of this second book is concerned with the analysis of the state of virtue as forming the middle state between two vices, excess and defect. This is the famous *mesotes* theory, which has exerted such a strong influence on ethical theories in general.

Aristotle rightly discovers the importance of the middle ground in various fields of human life. Too much food is as unhealthy as too little. In temperamental dispositions too-great loquacity is as unpleasant as too-great taciturnity. It is better that one have neither too much vivacity nor too little. In art, a work should be neither too long nor too short. But does this principle apply equally to the moral sphere?

The Aristotelian *mesotes* theory certainly contains an important truth concerning the moral sphere. It is a fact that there exists an objective proportion between the rank of a good and the nature of our response, that our response should be in conformity, in its intensity and depth, with the good on the object side. We can fail in overrating a good as well as in underrating it. One can, for instance, be too much concerned with one's health or one can care too little for it. The bureaucrat overrates the value of the juridical sphere, the bohemian or anarchist underrates it.

It is a fundamental moral principle that we should give every good the response which is due to it according to its rank, that it should play in our lives the role which corresponds to its objective value.

Unfortunately, Aristotle does not restrict his thesis to this important truth but tries to find the source of morality in a medium between excess and defect. He believes that every virtue lies between two vices, the one due to excess and the other to defect, whereas in reality the decisive factor dividing virtues and vices consists in whether the object motivating our attitude is endowed with an authentic value or whether it is merely subjectively satisfying.

Liberality differs from prodigality not because the prodigal gives too much but because the liberal spends his money for goods possessing an authentic value (such as support of the poor), whereas the prodigal spends his money in order to procure pleasures for himself. The main moral difference is whether the attitude is a value response or merely a response to something subjectively satisfying. Thus a prodigal man, if he becomes less and less prodigal until he becomes stingy and avaricious, will never on this road encounter the attitude of generosity. In reality, stinginess and prodigality are only two forms of one and the same basic attitude of concupiscence or selfishness, both equally opposed to generosity, which flows out of a pure value response.

Only when we have discovered that the main moral question is whether an attitude is a value response or not, does the aforementioned fact that every good possessing an authentic value calls for a response which is in conformity with its rank disclose itself in its true character.

Here again we encounter the truth which Aristotle has seen much more clearly than his main thesis expresses. He grants that some vices, such as malignity, impurity, envy and many others, cannot be explained by his *mesotes* theory, as it is obviously not the excess which makes them morally bad. They are intrinsically bad, and even the smallest portion of them is morally negative. But what is even more astonishing is that he reverses his own theory in Book IV, when he deals with the different virtues in detail. As soon as he is in direct contact with reality, his philosophical genius compels him to admit "that liberality differs above all from prodigality" because the money "is here spent for honorable things."

But notwithstanding this decisive insight, which we should expect to lead him to give up the *mesotes* theory, he again affirms this theory at the end, a typical example of the fact that the most valuable philosophical insights must not be sought in the main theses but in the single insights; we find these insights during the process of contacting reality, and sometimes indeed they are mentioned only in passing.

We shall find many such insights—they surpass and sometimes even reverse the over-all theory in this philosophical master-work—if we approach it with an attitude which does not seek for a system but rather to learn how much has been discovered in the concrete analysis.

As long as a pure value response is at stake—that is to say, as long as our interest in the object is exclusively motivated by its objective value—the response always will be adequate. When a response is inadequate, it is always due to the fact that some other elements appealing to our pride and concupiscence influence the motivation; thus our attitude is no longer a pure value response. Even though there is a necessary proportion between the response and the objective good, the morally decisive question remains: whether or not our response is exclusively motivated by authentic values.

Book VI is filled with most important insights. In the beginning we find the statement that certain organs correspond to certain objects, that is to say, the scientific organ is ordained toward the knowledge of invariable things, the calculative organ to the knowledge of the variables or contingent things.

Soon afterward we are struck by the insight that in the sphere of desire there also exists a ratio. This is expressed in the analogy between desiring and avoiding in the sphere of desire, and between affirmation and negation in the sphere of judgment. Moral virtue, based on deliberate choice, implies that the practical knowledge is true and the choice the right one, motivated by an authentic value.

But the most important discoveries are to be found in the analysis of the nature of practical wisdom.

First, we find in Chapter 5 the decisive statement: the knowledge of the right thing to choose in specific fields is not yet practical wisdom, but only the knowledge of a good life in general. This statement implies the distinction between practical knowledge concerning only the proper means for reaching an extramoral end, and the practical knowledge concerned with ends endowed with morally relevant values, though obviously Aristotle does not make this distinction explicitly.

In the following passages important insights abound. They cannot be read minutely enough. Here practical wisdom is clearly distinguished from science and art. The confusing analogy of morality with art which endangered in Book II the full understanding of the specific nature of morality is here completely eliminated.

In chapters 9 to 13 we find a further clarification of practical wisdom. The way in which practical wisdom is distinguished from scientific knowledge, from skill in conjecture and readiness of mind is a masterwork of phenomenological analysis. We should observe the method in its immediate, living, contact with the given data, the intuitive procedure, free from any arbitrary construction and abstract systemization. Aristotle states first that not every deliberation is yet practical wisdom. The evil man also can cleverly deliberate in order to attain his end. Yet true practical wisdom is only right reasoning directed to a good end. Aristotle clearly, though implicitly, sees that right deliberation assumes another character as soon as it is directed toward goods possessing an authentic value.

In the following distinction between practical wisdom and understanding as such, we find this important insight: true understanding merely leads to a right judgment, whereas practical wisdom, as concerned with that which ought to be, commands us to act in a certain way. Aristotle touches here the fundamental phenomenon of moral obligation and the role of conscience, as is revealed in his statement that as long as we judge other persons, it is merely understanding, whereas practical wisdom implies the experience of a moral obligation imposed on ourselves. We may say that practical wisdom is the grasping of the morally relevant value, as addressing itself to us in its obliging character. It is difficult to understand how Aristotle, with all these insights, never clearly grasped the nature of value as such, but always confused it with the notion of what is good for man.

In Chapter 12 arises the question: what is the value of practical wisdom, since it does not suffice to make us act in the right way, and since the good man does not seem to need practical wisdom. Aristotle answers by pointing out, first, that practical wisdom, as well as philosophical wisdom, has a value in itself independent of its use for morality, because it is an excellence of certain parts of the soul. Secondly—and here we reach the deepest and most important insight of this analysis—we have to distinguish between moral virtues in the broader sense of the word and moral virtues in the true and proper sense. As long as one acts in conformity with moral goodness, but makes one's choice not *because* of moral goodness, only virtue in the larger sense of the word is at stake. For true and authentic virtue, an intentional choice of the good *because* of its goodness is required. This choice, in its consciousness, implies practical wisdom, whereas virtue in the broader sense is unconscious.

In the concluding chapter Aristotle makes a masterly criticism of Socrates. He points out what Socrates saw rightly and where he went astray. In pretending that all moral virtues are only different forms of practical wisdom, Socrates erred. But in seeing that true moral virtue necessarily implies practical wisdom, he was right. He further erred in not distinguishing scientific knowledge and practical wisdom, and in claiming that moral virtue necessarily implies scientific knowledge.

This criticism of Socrates, besides having philosophical truth, also is a pattern of true and fruitful criticism and should be applied to our approach to Aristotle's philosophy itself. It does not presuppose that the work of a philosopher is a closed logical system in which we have to refute everything because the conclusion is wrong. It does, on the contrary, approach the thought of Socrates from the viewpoint of what Socrates has really discovered while in living contact with reality and where he fell into constructions.

This grand analysis concludes with the great truth: we cannot be morally good without practical wisdom, nor can we possess practical wisdom without being good.

DIETRICH VON HILDEBRAND

SELECTED BIBLIOGRAPHY

JAEGER, Werner, *Aristotle: Fundamentals of the History of His Development*. Oxford.
ROSS, W. D., *Aristotle*. London: Methuen.
ZELLER, E., *Aristotle and the Earlier Peripatetics*. Longmans, Green.
COPLESTON, Frederick, S.J., *A History of Philosophy* (Vol. I). Newman Bookshop.
ARISTOTLE, *Ethics*. Random (Modern Library).
ARISTOTLE, *Nicomachean Ethics*. Dutton (Everyman's Library).
ARISTOTLE, *Ethics*. Regnery.

Lucretius: On the Nature of Things,
Books I-IV

SINCE WE ordinarily think of Epicureanism as a system of ethics in which the supreme good is to be found in the excessive indulgence of the appetite for food and drink, it may come as a surprise to some readers of the *De Rerum Natura* of Lucretius to find that his work is an elaborate treatise on what the ancients called "physics" and later thinkers "cosmology." Time and the changing meanings of words have done a grave injustice to Epicurus: his ideal of "peace and tranquillity of mind and health of body" has been grossly distorted down the centuries. This very anomaly, however, brings us immediately to the heart of the system of Epicurus. Epicureanism was a philosophic quest for happiness in this life. Its protagonists, Epicurus and Lucretius, based their idea of what was morally good on their peculiar explanation of the nature of the physical world.

While the pre-Socratic philosophers of the Ionian coast turned to philosophizing in order to explain the visible phenomena that confronted them in their daily life (physics), and Plato turned inwardly, into the soul of man, to explore man's capabilities for virtue and education (ethics), Epicureanism pursued wisdom as a source of consolation for the trials and troubles of life and hence made physics the foundation stone of its system of ethics.

In the last century before the Christian era the shadowy figure of Lucretius looms as one of the greatest of the Roman poets. Fanatically devoted to his Greek predecessor, enthusiastic for his chosen philosophic theme, Lucretius combined a magnificent imagination with an orderly mind and a striking gift of poetic expression. The result is that his six books of Epicurean teaching draw a vivid picture of the man, of the decadent religion of the times and of the cravings for peace of mind, for which men looked in vain in the superficial schools of Roman thought.

The brilliant exposition of Lucretius portrays a soul tormented by fears and terrors and shocked by the evils that men do. With a vigorous and straightforward mind he dedicated himself to the task of freeing men from the worries that prevented them from achieving peace and happiness. The primary source of human misery lay in the terrible punishments that mythology held out for men in the lower world after death. How could a man be happy in this life when all he had to look forward to was an eternity of capricious and cruel torment? This terrifying prospect was for Lucretius the root and source of all the cruelty, injustice, murder and infidelity in the world, and since all these evils thus stemmed from "religion," it was obvious to him that the chains which bound men to the gods had to be broken.

This he found to have been done by Epicurus, whose atomic materialism obviated any need for the "gods" as creators of the universe or as the source of any reward or punishment in the life to come. The deism of Epicurus and Lucretius portrays the gods as living a life of peace and ease, far from the concerns of man, selfishly enjoying their own happiness, interested neither in man's sins nor in his virtues and altogether incapable of doing anything about them, even if they wished to do so. Lucretius aimed to persuade men that there could be no torment after death because the soul is mortal and at death was resolved back into its constituent atoms. With the dissolution of personality, existence was terminated, and what does not exist cannot suffer. Drawing strength from these assurances, he hoped to devote his life to the enjoyment of Epicurean calm and tranquillity.

The basis for all this lay in the fact that all reality is composed of atoms and void. The atoms he describes as hard, impenetrable, indestructible, everlasting, unchangeable and microscopic mites of matter, which whirled around in the limitless void of space. In the beginning there was merely the rain of atoms falling downward because of their weight; from the moment when two atoms met in collision, there ensued an infinite series of such blows and clashes as to result in the union of atoms, which ultimately brought about the formation of all things. Thus, no intelligent Mind guided the creation of the universe—all was the result of pure chance. Not only did things begin by such chance meetings of atoms, but in the same fashion the earth, with all its flora and fauna, continually reproduces itself.

Here we have the basic principle of the system: the impossibility of creation out of nothing. From his attempt to prove this point, we get some idea of Lucretius' notion of creation. Within the Lucretian universe there is law without any directing Mind; there is sequence of source and result without any causative influence. This very regularity and predictability made it obvious that there had been no divine influence. If the gods were at all concerned in creation and particularly in the conservation of things, all would happen irregularly, unpredictably, according to mere whim and impulse. "Divine" for Lucretius means "capricious."

Further, on the dissolution of any particular being, whether animal, vegetable or mineral, there was no annihilation of the atoms of which it has been composed. Death is merely the separation of the accidentally formed unions of the atoms which, when joined together, made up this or that man, plant or stone. The atoms alone, of all the universe, enjoyed immortality.

The specific nature of any single thing was merely the result of this chance collocation of atoms; sweet and smooth things were made up of round and polished atoms; rough and unpleasant things were the result of the union of spiked and hooked atoms. Soft things contained a larger percentage of void intermingled with their atoms than did hard and resistant materials.

A second cardinal principle of the Lucretian system is that whatever happens, happens because of the physical contact of atoms upon atoms, and this is the basis of his discussion of the nature and functioning of the soul. The soul's atoms are the roundest, smoothest and most speedily mobile of all the elements of the universe, and whatever sensation or idea is conceived in the human soul must take place by the physical impact of the atoms of the thing known upon the atoms of the soul. Thus we are able to see, because there is continually streaming away from the surface of all things a layer of atoms, a kind of filmy outline, an image (*simulacrum*) of the body. These impinge upon the eye, and we see the object. Our perception of the distance of the object is a marvelous and momentary evaluation of this impact, which tells us how far away the object lies. So likewise we hear, by the physical contact of the atoms of sound upon our ears, and so of the other senses.

While Lucretius demands the existence of atoms as the foundation of his universe, it is to be noted that he cannot offer any positive proof that there really are such atoms, but he has to fall back on the analogy of our sense perception of other things which we cannot see but which we know from their effects. Therefore, he is absolutely convinced of the infallibility of the senses. For him, sense knowledge is the criterion of truth; where the senses seem to fail (optical illusions), it is really the mind that makes the error.

The mind is a part of the soul and resides in the breast; the functioning of the mind is essentially the same as that of the senses. Some atoms there are that are so fine and mobile that they make no impression on the senses, but the more sensitive soul is able to grasp them. Whatever we "think of" is the result of such a meeting between the atoms of the soul and a *simulacrum*. Since the *simulacra* are infinite, there are enough of them to give us the impression that we can, at times, deliberately choose to think of something new. The idea we have of an impossible thing, such as a centaur, is the result of the chance meeting of *simulacra* or "idols" of a man and a horse. Thus also are formed dreams: while we sleep, wandering idols attach themselves to the atoms of the mind; movement of the objects of our dreams is an illusion produced by the rapid succession in which almost identical idols touch the soul. When, in his dreams, Lucretius "saw" people who were already dead (and, on his theory, no longer existent) he was in stark terror of an event he could not explain, for any *simulacrum* had to be emitted by an existing body. From the number of times he comes back to this matter of dreams, we can see that he conceived a rankling suspicion that perhaps souls did continue to exist after death.

His third principle is that the soul must be mortal, else the whole structure of his system is in vain. To prove this essential point, Lucretius calls upon all the resources of his imagination and his powers of persuasion in his twenty-eight arguments for the mortality of the soul. The basic principle of them all is that the soul is composed of atoms and therefore: a) it is divisible and can be broken down; b) it is capable of internal development and increases in size with the body, hence it must be capable

of deterioration and death; c) it can be changed by outside in-
fluences such as food and drink, and sickness of the body weighs
it down; d) it can neither exist nor function independently of
the body, but on separation from the body it will dissolve into
the breezes of the air.

Triumphant at having established this point to his satisfaction,
Lucretius launches into the finest portion of his poem when, in
impassioned eloquence, he pleads with men to believe him; with
masterful irony, he scorns the thoughts which men in their weakness entertain of all they will be deprived of after death. Kings
and poets, heroes and philosophers, even the divine Epicurus—
all have died and no man ever escapes this dissolution. But death
is really nothing to be feared, because nothing can happen to you
when you no longer exist. How can a man "miss" the love of his
wife and children when there will be no feeling of any kind?
It is one of the supreme anomalies of the mind of Lucretius that
such complete destruction of personality appeared to him the
greatest boon of consolation ever offered to poor suffering
humanity.

Thus the essential elements of his theory are completed in
the first four books of his work. The remainder serves to gather
together the loose ends of natural phenomena for which men,
in their fear, sought an explanation. On the basis of his atomic
theory Lucretius explains the motion of the stars and the planets,
the origin of earthquakes and storms, the beginnings and development of all forms of life and of human society. These
matters, however, introduce no new principles, but merely
reiterate his fourth idea, which has been implicit in all he has
said, namely, that there is no such thing as causality. We were
not endowed with eyes by some intelligent creator in order that
we may be able to see; but rather, eyes (and everything else) having been formed by the chance meeting of atoms, men learned
in time that they could be used for sight. So likewise of every
other faculty that we possess. He is, of course, forced into this
position by his initial postulate, that there can be no intelligent
guidance behind the order that is apparent in the universe.

So great was the emotional impulse that continually drove
Lucretius and fed his zeal as the apostle of the gospel according
to Epicurus, that he seems generally unaware of the weakness of

his basic principles. Thus we have seen that his only demonstration of the existence of atoms and void is a weak argument from analogy. He could not, in his age, see with his eyes the atoms and their movements, and so he advances a series of "arguments" as to the effect of the wind, odors, moisture, growth and decay, which take place even though we cannot see them. All this merely proves that there *might be* atoms, but the leap from what might be to what actually was, presented no difficulties for the agile mind of Lucretius.

Dependent on that first principle, is his second—the impossibility of any perception without contact. For if there is nothing but atoms in anything, there can be no union without contact. If everything is made up of atoms, the soul also must be composed of material atoms and any union of atoms will ultimately be broken down. Since there is no need of an intelligent creator (all happens by chance) there could be no teleology, or rational adaptation of means to end. There we have the basic contradiction of his whole system: inexorable law and regularity without any mind to conceive or guide the operation of the wondrous universe with which he was entranced.

Important as all these weaknesses are, however, there is one other principle for which Lucretius offers not a scintilla of proof and without which his whole universe will never even get started. It will be remembered that in the beginning there were an infinite number of atoms falling downward in the void. Since they were falling in a vacuum, he realized that the different weights of atoms would not cause them to fall faster or slower: hence there never would be any contact or collisions, but all would fall interminably in the void without ever meeting. In a desperate attempt to obviate this difficulty, he introduces "the swerve of the atoms," which would cause them to fall sideways and hence start the infinity of blows which would bring about union and the production of material things. This uncaused "swerve" is also alleged as the source of free will in men and animals, by which they appear to determine of themselves what they will do. To this, one might reply that the swerve will not help if *all atoms fall on the bias* (which is what he says) but that the slightest inclination of even *a single atom* would ultimately bring about the desired effect. But, once again, his mere wish that there *be* a swerve was sufficient to prove to Lucretius that *there really was one*.

If Lucretius the philosopher is the victim of his emotions and his perfervid imagination, these very qualities enabled him to write the story of his sorrows and of his attempt to win freedom from their torment in what is one of the most beautiful poems of all literature. Even in his most involved theoretical passages, the poet's eye ranged the universe from end to end and "beyond the flaming ramparts of the world" to encompass all reality; if he saw no gods seated on the Olympian heights, he there built a throne for the only god he recognized, his guide and master, Epicurus. The zeal and enthusiasm he manifests was worthy of a better cause: from the knowledge of the man that we glean from his poem, it would seem likely he would have embraced Christianity with enthusiasm if he could have known of a God of Love who called to Himself "all you that labor and are heavily burdened."

But Lucretius sought for consolation where it never can be found—in a materialism that denies the possibility of the supernatural and the spiritual. Lucretius, as does every materialist, opened his eyes and refused to look at *all* that lay before him. Inevitably his quest for truth and happiness was foredoomed to despairing failure. It seems likely that his didactic zeal was, first and foremost, aimed at himself, trying to persuade Lucretius to be a convinced and tranquil Epicurean. In that, he failed—the misery of his life caused him to die by his own hand.

It is perhaps not without some significance in our times that the high priest of modern (dialectical) materialism, Karl Marx, wrote his dissertation for the doctorate from the University of Jena on Lucretius and his atomic predecessors, Epicurus and Democritus. Marx would seem to have been attracted to the subject by his own hatred of religion. In the foreword of the book, he used as his own the motto of Aeschylus' Prometheus: "In one word, I hate all the gods."

EDWIN A. QUAIN

SELECTED BIBLIOGRAPHY

BAILEY, Cyril, *Lucretius on the Nature of Things* (translation). Oxford.
BAILEY, Cyril, *The Greek Atomists and Epicurus.* Oxford.
HADZITS, R. D., *Lucretius and His Influence.* Boston: Marshall Jones.
MASSON, John, *Lucretius, Epicurean and Poet* (2 Vols.). London: John Murray.
HICKS, R. D., *Stoic and Epicurean.* Scribner.
LUCRETIUS, *On the Nature of Things.* Dutton (Everyman's Library).
LUCRETIUS, *On the Nature of Things.* Regnery.

Marcus Aurelius: Meditations

WHAT THE emperor Marcus Aurelius achieved during the years of his remarkable reign (161-180 A.D.) perished with the Roman Empire, but the philosopher Marcus Aurelius lives on in his *Reflections,* or *Meditations,* a book which has become a part of the world's great literature. Through its translation from the original Greek into practically every civilized language it has provided comfort and strength to uncounted numbers of men. Nor is there missing a true likeness of the outward appearance of the philosopher-king on the throne of the Roman Caesars, for a friendly fate has preserved from destruction his famous equestrian statue. During the Middle Ages it stood near the Lateran and was, as the inscription records, transferred to the Piazza del Campidoglio (Square of the Capitol) in 1538, where it was placed on its present pedestal. The rider sits well on his horse, extending his right hand in a simple gesture of serene authority, as if addressing the subjects of his wide realm.

Looking down from his pedestal, the once gilded, now patina-green emperor has witnessed a considerable part of world history. He has seen the temples of the ancient gods fall to pieces while Christian churches arose and were often laid in ruins again. Goths, Vandals, Heruli, Byzantines, Normans, Saracens, knights and their retainers, armies of the German emperors and papal troops, French and Spanish, Republicans and Monarchists, Socialists and Fascists have marched past him but, like that of a true Stoic philosopher, his serene countenance has never changed.

Marcus Aurelius' ancestors had come from Spain to Rome and there became members of the senatorial order. He himself was born at Rome in 121 A.D. and after the early death of his father was adopted by his grandfather. At the beginning of the first book of his *Meditations* he acquaints us with his family. He describes his grandfather as a man of kindly disposition; his father, according to what he had heard of him, as a model of modesty and manliness, and his mother as a god-fearing lady, full of generosity, who taught her son to live a simple life, far removed from the habits of the rich.

The youth soon gained the favor of Hadrian (117-138 A.D.) who, following the second-century method of securing a capable successor on the imperial throne, adopted Antoninus Pius (138-161 A.D.) on the condition that he in turn adopt Marcus Aurelius. Thus Marcus Aninus Verus—for this was his original name—scion of a senatorial family, was destined in his early youth to be seated, in due time, on the throne of the Roman Caesars, though his meditative disposition inclined him to quite a different life.

In the house of his grandfather he received an excellent education by the outstanding teachers of the time. Education by private tutors seems to have been a family custom. As Marcus Aurelius tells us, his grandfather's father did not think too highly of the public schools of the time, but preferred to employ good teachers at home, thinking such money well spent. In the first book of his *Meditations* we learn not only the names of Marcus Aurelius' numerous private tutors but as well the contribution which each of them made to his education.

The Stoic Diognetus was the first to acquaint him with philosophy. When he was about twenty, Cornelius Fronto and Herodes Atticus took great pains to interest their imperial pupil in rhetoric. However, to the great disappointment of Fronto, the influence of the Stoic Junius Rusticus, who gave him the works of Epictetus to read, resulted in his bidding farewell to all those literary aspirations which concentrated too one-sidedly on the merely esthetic aspects of literature. Though he had become familiar with the teachings of the Platonic, Peripatetic and Stoic schools of philosophy, it was only the last which was capable of stirring and satisfying his great soul. What Marcus would have become, had he not been the heir presumptive of imperial Rome, can only be guessed: perhaps a brooding theorist or a head of the Stoic school or one of its itinerant preachers and propagandists. The force of circumstances did not allow him to embrace philosophy as a vocation.

Nevertheless, it was philosophy that molded his character and gave him strength and guidance throughout his life. In his *Medi-*

tations he compares the imperial court with a stepmother, and philosophy with one's own mother. Though one has to pay due service to the former, it is to the latter that one has constant recourse. It was therefore in her that the emperor often took his rest, it was she who made court life more tolerable to him (6.12). He wished to become on the throne what philosophy wished to make of him: "Remember that philosophy wishes but what thy nature wishes . . . high-mindedness, independence, simplicity, kindness of heart, piety" (5.9).

With Marcus Aurelius the peaceful period in the history of the Roman Empire, known as the *Pax Romana,* came to an end. It fell to the last of the so-called good emperors of the second century to spend the greater part of his reign in the field, defending the Empire against attacks from all sides. In the East it was the Parthians who attacked the southeastern provinces of the Empire. Fortunately, Marcus had at his disposal an extremely capable general, Avidius Cassius, who successfully handled this most difficult campaign. However, the army brought back from the East a plague which raged for years in Italy and some of the provinces.

In the West it was the northern barbarians who fell on the Danube frontier with terrific force, one wave of them rolling as far as the Italian frontier and reaching Aquileia. In this critical situation the emperor shouldered the burden himself, marching against the invaders and driving them back beyond the Danube. Military complications in Africa and Egypt and a frightful mutiny headed by Avidius Cassius in Syria prevented him from exploiting his victories. He had not yet put down these new dangers when war broke out again on the Danube. Marcus Aurelius did not live to see its end, for he died during the campaign near Vienna in 180 A.D.

All during this time the resources of the Empire were strained to the utmost by the constant wars. Against his will the emperor had had to increase taxation. In order to raise funds, he had even sold the imperial jewels. The tremendous weight of responsibility placed on his shoulders was doubly felt by him since he could expect little, if any, assistance from his coregent, the easy-going Lucius Verus. Nor could his own choice of a successor have brought him much comfort. Ignoring the above-mentioned second-century method of succession, which consisted in a combination of free selection with adoption, he had designated his own son Commodus to be his successor. No one knew better than Marcus that Commodus was unfitted for the task, but natural affection and domestic influence had been too strong for him.

In his *Meditations* (4.3) Marcus Aurelius counsels that man constantly retreat into himself, because nowhere can he find a retreat more full of peace or more free from care than his own soul. This continual retirement effects, too, a continual regeneration of oneself. This counsel was no empty talk: the emperor himself was guided by it. His *Diary* resulted from notes or memoranda which he jotted down late in the evening after winding up government business, or in camp during his campaigns against the Germanic tribes on the Danube. In this way there came into existence Books II to XII, while the first book was written last and prefixed as a kind of introduction to the whole work. *Reflections,* or *Meditations,* is the title by which it is known. However, this is not the name which he gave to it himself. He called it *Eis Heautón—To Himself*. As a ruler he took counsel with himself so that he might be able to act "as only a good man should in the strictest sense of that word" (4.10). Thus his *Meditations* give us an insight into his noble mind as well as into the principles which guided him in his actions. Man became, as hardly ever before, the central point of a literary work, and in this sense the "self-contemplation" of Marcus Aurelius may be considered a forerunner of St. Augustine's *Confessions* or *Soliloquies*.

Marcus Aurelius admires and reveres the cosmos, the universe, as an embodiment of order and harmony, the one nature which, permeated by one divine Reason, is the maternal womb which gives birth to all things. As a result, all things are mutually intertwined, like to one another and bound by sacred ties (4.14; 6.38; 7.9). Man is also a part of the cosmos. Though a very small part, he is particularly valuable because of his reason which is an efflux of the divine. As a matter of fact, Marcus is interested in the cosmos for the very reason that man is in it.

Of the three parts of which man consists, namely, body, soul and reason (cf. 2.2; 3.16; 6.32; 12.3), the last rouses his special interest because it is "the most excellent thing" in man and, being the seat of right understanding, independence and justice, must govern his life (5.21). "Every hour," Marcus writes, "form unfalteringly the resolution as a Roman and a man to do thy daily work with scrupulousness, unaffected dignity, love of mankind, independence, and justice, and not to allow any other thought to spring up in thy mind. Thou wilt be able to do this, if thou dost execute every act as if it were the last of thy life, ridding thyself of all thoughtlessness and all passionate antipathy to the guidance of reason, and all hypocrisy and selfishness and grudge against thy lot" (2.5). Reason is such a precious gift because man shares it with the gods. Therefore, no harm can come from a work which has been accomplished in obedience to that reason (7.53).

Within the never-ceasing revolution of all things, which takes place in recurring cycles of enormous length, Marcus Aurelius emphasizes the conservation of matter and elements, the continuous renewal of things and the superiority of all-embracing nature over revolution. Nevertheless, nothing made a deeper impression on him than the transitoriness of all things earthly. With this thought he connects a second one: all is vanity; man, having subsisted but as a part of the whole, will vanish into that which begat him, or rather will be taken again into its seminal Reason by a process of change. All that man values so highly in his life is empty, rotten and worthless (cf. 4.3; 5; 14; 5.33).

One would think this contempt of all things earthly would necessarily lead to pessimism, since man himself, after a brief journey on this earth, is taken back into the eternal Reason which contains the seed of all things. There was no room for immortality in the Stoic scheme. Marcus Aurelius tried to overcome this difficulty by pointing to man's task within the universe. All creatures have to follow the way marked out for them by divine Providence. By accomplishing their tasks within their own limited sphere, they contribute to the harmony in the universe (5.8; 6.11). Man has to contribute his share in the building up of an harmonious universe. Every morning he should rise with the thought that he has to accomplish a man's work, to do that for which he was born and had come into this world (5.1). Everything else should be of no concern to him, nor should anything else trouble his mind. And this, his task, man can fulfil in spite of the vicissitudes of life and the evil existing in the world. For he can never be prevented from making full use of his reason. This is in accord with the divine will. This also is what Marcus means by "living according to nature" (cf. 1.9; 1.17; 5; 2.9; 4.39; 48; 51; 5.3; 9; 6.40; 58); he does not approve the rather materialistic sense in which the Cynics employed that phrase; for nature too is God.

We have to keep in mind that to Marcus Aurelius, the Stoic and pantheist, God and the universe were identical, "one living Being possessed of a single substance and a single soul" (4.40). All-wise nature is also all-virtuous, doing only what is best and never sending anything that man cannot bear (5.18; 8.46; 10.3). In simple obedience and with a humble heart, therefore, man should say to nature: "Give what thou wilt, take back what thou wilt" (10.14).

By taking such an attitude, Marcus Aurelius personally accomplished what he considered to be man's task in this world, namely, to live decently and to die bravely—for death too is a task which man should perform well. When life's journey comes to an end, he should depart with a cheerful mind, "just as an olive falls when it has become ripe, praising the earth which brought it forth, and grateful to the tree which gave it growth" (4.48). One cannot but admire the brave spirit which manifests itself in this interpretation of human life.

And yet one wonders why this man who shows so great a contempt for all things earthly and such a great esteem for man's rational faculties, did not attempt to gain a deeper insight into the religious philosophy of Platonism in order to supply the defects in his own philosophy of life. Thus there remained a wide gulf between his lofty conception of the self-conscious human personality and his Stoic idea of the impersonal, immanent world force, or world soul, which could be envisaged under many aspects and names—Destiny, God, Providence, the Universal Law, the All, the Reason of the Universe, Truth, Nature. On the one hand, the individual man was but one of the countless fragments that made up the divine Being. On the other hand, this divine Being was impersonal. Therefore, no single part of it could validly claim personality. As a further result, the ancient problem of happiness remained unsolved because Stoicism necessarily led to a fatalistic and stunned acquiescence in life. Stoicism could perhaps be a source of solace and strength to such extraordinary and noble individuals as Marcus Aurelius, but it was never able to satisfy man's ever-clamoring desire for personal happiness beyond the grave.

There is something else which makes a deep impression on the reader of the *Meditations:* its deeply religious tone. Marcus Aurelius must have been a sincerely devout man, as his frequent references to prayer show. Moreover, he likes to dwell on the thought of man's kinship with God. The idea of the human mind being "a particle" of Zeus himself, the divine "genius" (*daimon*) within man and his appointed "captain and guide" (3.3; 5.27), forms the bridge between religious and merely ethical duties. Anyone who opposes this genius by disobedience to his laws—which are but those of reason—commits a sacrilege against the deity. In this way all infringements of the moral law become acts of impiety (cf. 2.13; 16; 17; 3.16; 5.27), and the necessity of religion as a basis for morality is recognized.

The *Meditations* contain still some other most appealing ideas, namely, those of one brotherhood of man under the fatherhood of God, of brotherly love and of forbearance (cf. 2.1; 16; 4.3.2; 8.8; 9.42). Such thoughts were not new. They had been expressed before by Seneca and Epictetus, and were based on the Stoic idea of the communion of all men as rational beings and as citizens of a world state within which the single states have the same function as the single households within a city (cf. 3.11.2; 4.4). What gives the sentences of Marcus Aurelius their enduring value and places them above the theoretical utterances of Seneca and Epictetus is that they became the gospel of his life.

The king-philosopher made the sincere and courageous attempt to base his rule on the principles of his philosophy, and to practice the virtues he extols in his *Diary*. For this, all the more credit must be given him, since during his reign the Roman Empire was beset by misfortunes of all kinds: from without there were formidable attacks by enemies, within the threatened frontiers there were floods, famines and pestilence. By nature neither a general nor a statesman, he shouldered this burden with his characteristic sense of duty. He may have been excelled in warfare by more than one of his commanders in the field, he may have given orders which harmed the very interest of the state, yet there can be no doubt of his justice, his humane disposition, and his solicitude for the well-being of his subjects, manifested especially in the administration of finance and law. It was in the treatment of his enemies especially that his noble-mindedness shone forth most beautifully, returning love for hatred, good for evil.

Plato had expressed the idea that, unless philosophers became rulers, or rulers true philosophers, there would be no end to the troubles of states and humanity. In the person of Marcus Aurelius a true philosopher had ascended the throne. But it was just this king-philosopher who demonstrated that Plato's idea was unrealizable. Plato demanded too much from philosophy. Philosophical excellence does not yet guarantee excellence in the domains of practical life. Marcus Aurelius knew too well that even a ruler whose actions were guided by the best intentions was unable to make straight all crooked paths. It was from this experience that he wrote: "Do not hope for the ideal state of Plato, but be content if there is an improvement in the most insignificant thing" (9.29).

It is a strange historical coincidence that, during the reign of the best of all "good" emperors, persecutions of Christians sprang up again in different parts of the Empire. It is to be regretted that Marcus Aurelius, who had a passion for justice, did not understand Christianity. In vain Christian apologists tried to get the ear of the philosopher, but they found that they were dealing with a man who was all the more inflexible because he was so conscientious.

Though Stoicism, in a final effort of the pagan mind to create a system of morals acceptable to all men, could win only a very small minority to its standard, it actually created a few chosen men of great courage, integrity and good will. Marcus Aurelius was one of the few. Many ethical writings of antiquity may be more learned, but none of them equals his *Meditations* in moral seriousness and intrinsic value.

RUDOLPH ARBESMANN

SELECTED BIBLIOGRAPHY

BUSSELL, F. W., *Marcus Aurelius and the Later Stoics*. Scribner.
DAVIS, Ch. H. St., *Greek and Roman Stoicism and Some of Its Disciples: Epictetus, Seneca, and Marcus Aurelius*. Boston: H. B. Turner.
SEDGWICK, H. D., *Marcus Aurelius*. Yale University.
AURELIUS, *Meditations*. Dutton (Everyman's Library).
AURELIUS, *Meditations*. Regnery.

Hobbes: Leviathan

THOMAS HOBBES's *Leviathan,* published in 1651 when its author was sixty-three years old, constitutes the third attempt of the man whom G. P. Gooch has called "the most original and the least English of the three great [English] political thinkers" to formulate a political philosophy. *Leviathan* has become Hobbes's best-known work, though the most recent authoritative interpreter of Hobbes, Leo Strauss, claims that it is "by no means an adequate source for an understanding of Hobbes's moral and political ideas."

Hobbes's thought developed slowly. The son of a minister, he was born in 1588 and was educated at Oxford, where he became an enemy of an incompetently presented Aristotle and a decadent scholasticism. At the age of nineteen he entered the services of the Cavendish family, whose head had been elevated to nobility with the title of Earl of Devonshire. This connection lasted for seventy years, until Hobbes's death in 1679; some interruptions there were, but they did not result in a definitive break. Hobbes had ample opportunity to observe life in the good society. For a time he served as a kind of secretary to Bacon, and he spent eleven years as a voluntary exile in France.

These experiences resulted in a not-too-flattering opinion of human nature: men are selfish and are determined in their relations to each other by egoism and vanity. When he was forty years old Hobbes became impressed by the rigid character of mathematical proofs discovered in Euclid. But the scientific-mathematical method which he emphasizes in his works is only a form to present his psychological experiences and his utilitarian beliefs. It is self-evident to Hobbes that the end of man is to enjoy life as much and as long as possible. Lack of moderation, excesses and overestimations of power caused by too much pride, vainglory and vanity must result in self-destruction. These passions or motions are opposed by countermotions caused by the fear of death, by man's longing for external peace and security. Reason is for Hobbes a means for ordering man's sensual experiences, for building up his life as a mechanism which will run satisfactorily, making enjoyment of pleasures possible by helping to avoid a premature death.

This description of man's nature from the point of view of Hobbes's materialistic-mechanistic philosophy forms the first part of the *Leviathan*, entitled "Of Man." The second part, "Of Commonwealth," deals with the mechanism, the artificial body of the commonwealth, united and kept alive by the will of the sovereign. This mechanism is necessary in order to solve the conflict in man between the two basic motions, destructive vainglory and pride on the one side, and the desire for a long, secure, peaceful life on the other. The external and overwhelming power of the sovereign prevents men from killing each other; it imposes upon them laws which make possible a life without constant threat of violent death and with commercial and civilizatory progress.

The indivisible and unlimited power of the sovereign is further characterized in parts III and IV of the *Leviathan*. These sections show that the sovereign must control religion. In the "Christian Commonwealth," with which Part III deals, there must be complete subservience of religious rules and organizations to the will of the sovereign. The visible kingdom of God must be completely dominated by the rulers on earth. Part IV characterizes the church of the Roman popes as the "Kingdom of Darkness"; the papacy is attacked as "the ghost of deceased Roman Empire sitting crowned upon the grave thereof." The authority of the popes is for Hobbes based upon deception of the people, provoked by fear of excommunication, etc. Thomas Hobbes's hate of the Catholic Church is but an expression of his general belief that all religious institutions and doctrines ought to be under the authority and control of the sovereign. He hates Puritans as much as Catholics, accusing them of establishing their domination by creating feelings of guilt.

Hobbes's political philosophy is developed positively in the first two parts of the *Leviathan* and negatively, in the form of attacks against claims of religion for independence, in the last two parts. It aims to present the blueprint for a mechanism which would overcome destructive human passions and therefore establish a reasonable, lasting, pleasant life. Hobbes is interested in describing the conditions under which peace and security demanded by natural law can be realized. Under natural law he understands necessary rules for a long and progressive life in this world. Realization of peace and security will end a state of nature in which men necessarily fight and destroy each other.

In this state Hobbes's famous *bellum omnium contra omnes* ("a warre, as of every man against every man") prevails because passions are not checked "by a common power to keep them all in awe." Therefore men must fight each other. The state of nature is for Hobbes a state in which a sovereign with overwhelming power does not exist. It does not matter for him if this state of nature has been observed in history, or if it is only an abstraction conceived in order to explain the necessity and the functioning of society, made possible only by the existence of the sovereign. The sovereign ends the war—characteristic for the state of nature—and establishes peace and security by backing up social relations and contracts with his force, against which successful resistance is impossible. "Covenants without the sword are but words, and of no strength to secure a man at all."

The sovereign represents each individual—his authority came into being (or at least must be explained) as the result of a decision of each individual which gives the right to act in his own name to the sovereign—provided that all other individuals do the same. Therefore the unity of the commonwealth is not based upon relations among individuals or the existence of the will of a multitude, but exclusively upon the will of the sovereign. If the sovereign disappears, society disappears too. The sovereign has no obligations to his subjects. If he could be taken to account by them as partner of a contract, he would not be the supreme power holding society together and protecting it by his strength. The power of the sovereign cannot be divided or limited. If that were done, the commonwealth would cease to exist, the state of society would return to the state of nature.

It does not matter for Hobbes if the sovereign is one man or a multitude—what matters is the necessity that the sovereign power is supreme and unchallengeable. The justification is a utilitarian one. Hobbes cannot be regarded as a defender of legitimate monarchy or of the divine right of kings. The sovereign is necessary in order to protect against violent death and constant insecurity. If he is unable to protect, any obligation toward him ceases. Hobbes accepted Cromwell's rule in 1651, for he believed that the cause of the monarchy had suffered a defeat beyond repair, though earlier he had been an adherent of the Stuarts. Later on, he was glad to be favored by Charles II after the Restoration.

The sovereign must be able to impose his will. He ought to do it in a reasonable way, in a way which does not destroy its own power by provoking rebellion through excesses. The self-interest of the sovereign alone can protect against tyrannical rule. He alone can realize the welfare of the people. The subjects have no right to rebellion, for rebellion results in a return to the state of nature, to a civil war characterized by threats of violent death and insecurity. Hobbes is an enemy of churchmen who accept the right of resistance. He is against members of the parliament who destroy sovereignty by trying to divide and to limit it. He is against jurists and judges who do not realize that the sovereign cannot be challenged in the name of the common law, which he has established.

But Hobbes's sovereign is not a tyrant regarding constant expansion of his power as the end of his rule. The famous description of the life under the state of nature as being nasty, brutish, short, without art, science, commerce, shows clearly that the sovereign of Hobbes is not a totalitarian ruler eager to control all realms of life, from music to economics. The sovereign of Hobbes makes commerce and science possible. Under his protection they can fully and freely develop. But there are no individual and social rights which can be invoked against the sovereign, for acceptance of such rights would destroy the basic right of men to exist in peace and security. Hobbes assumes that the sovereign will be interested in establishing legal security, protecting private property (which became possible only after the end of the state of nature) and not destroying it: it is for a sovereign more profitable to become rich by collecting taxes than to destroy his own profits by confiscation of his subjects' property.

This political philosophy which reduces the relation between authority and subjects to a power relation based upon utilitarian calculation—without the sovereign there is no peace and security—cannot develop an understanding of religion. Religion is for Hobbes the result of human fear and of the necessity to find an ultimate explanation for the chain of causes. That is clearly expressed in a comparison of religious beliefs with pills which are "wholesome—swallowed whole, but chewed without effect." Religion fulfils for Hobbes simply a psychological function, giving consolation to men, explaining mysterious aspects of life, and justifying the power of the sovereign. Religious organizations are praised if they help the power of the sovereign.

Religious teaching is reduced to the obligation to obey unquestionably and gladly the orders of the sovereign; God's will is the will of the earthly sovereign. Religion is accepted as a utilitarian psychological force but not as a truth. Of course Hobbes is afraid to express these views too openly and directly. They are hidden behind apparently fideistic statements—about God, whose nature cannot be known, about a revelation which is so absolutely separated from reason that its truth cannot be grasped by men, and by an astonishing facility for misinterpreting the Bible.

Hobbes's political philosophy is based upon his views of nature and man. Nature and man he regards as complexes of motions regulated either by themselves or by artificial means invented by human reason (that is, by the artificial mechanism of the commonwealth). His political philosophy corresponds to a particular development in modern history. It tries to liberate the rising modern state from all limitations by forces which he regards as purely external limitations, no longer corresponding to the modern élite of businessmen and scientists. The Church, and Protestant groups which also argue that the state cannot claim all power for itself alone and which ascribe to men an end to life beyond the "race" here on earth, are regarded as enemies.

Hobbes tries to show that the earthly society must dominate the whole life. Its sovereign establishes peace and security. Secondly, Hobbes's views correspond to those rather pessimistic, naturalistic views on human nature which are attractive to men who have ample opportunities to observe human maneuvers and vanities in social life, "the market friendships," the gossip about those who are absent in order to present their own superiority, the shameless respect for power and success. Thirdly, Hobbes's philosophy is strongly individualistic—profit for the individual is the leading motive of human behavior. This individualism is expressed in a mechanistic approach which brings the individual units together and explains why their external unification is at the same time necessary and useful, in harmony with natural-mechanical laws of motion.

Hobbes's philosophy must be regarded as a classical example of basic errors. Hobbes replaces reality with a mass of sensual impressions. The nature of reason is misunderstood—reason is simply a means for combinations and knowledge of the sequence of impressions. The highest form of knowledge is for Hobbes the capacity to construe blueprints for social mechanisms which will prevent the destructive working of passions and which will bring, by external compulsion, order into their movements. The end of human life is a purely immanent one—there is no higher end beyond death—and if there is an immortality, then it is only the immortality of the functioning social mechanism, of the sovereign power of the Leviathan which survives its individual bearers as well as its subject, for it is grounded upon eternal social-mechanical laws.

The social nature of men is completely overlooked. Hobbes's man does not know love or hate, he knows only well- or badly-calculated self-interest. Hobbes's man is not a mysterious being who participates in the world of angels as well as of beasts, but a mechanism only somewhat complicated by his possession of the power to calculate and anticipate. The living reality is degraded to a world of mechanical relations. These deficiencies are hidden behind a suggestive and brilliant style and unforgettable, sharp formulas.

Hobbes's *Leviathan* is, despite its fundamental errors, a great book—for it formulates its basic views with extraordinary force and suggestive clarity, and has therefore become a classic expression of a thought combining utilitarian individualism with an attempt to justify a strong sovereign power. Hobbes can therefore be characterized as an ancestor of modern liberalism as well as of totalitarianism.

A quiet despair casts its shadow over the work of Hobbes. The basic views appear realistic because they oppose a cheap idealism and a sentimental rhetoric which do not dare to face the facts of power and the reality of human nature. Human nature is neither bad nor good, though it threatens itself with destruction by not realizing its own self-interest. It is the decisive defect of Hobbes that his opposition against the shortcomings of those who overlooked the utilitarian and passionate (irrational) aspects of human nature made him accept a view of man which makes man a part of a universal mechanism, though able by his reason to balance his passions and utilize them for social, cultural, industrial, commercial progress.

Hobbes is a cynic; but he believes at the same time in a world in which business ranks highest—business which makes life comfortable and develops, with the help of scientific, technical discoveries and with the help of competition kept within limits by the rules of the sovereign, a steadily progressing society. Hobbes's society is not a society of men but an inhuman mechanism, a Leviathan protecting external security though not aware that there is a good life beyond the satisfaction of utilitarian needs and that there is knowledge greater than the capacity to develop blueprints.

But the fearless logic with which Hobbes, from questionable premises, develops his thought, makes his best-known book, *Leviathan,* a Great Book which continues an old individualist-utilitarian tradition (opposed by Plato's *Republic*) into the modern age. Hobbes is the philosopher of a world dominated by utilitarian businessmen who believe in an eternal progress of technical civilization. His totalitarian *Leviathan* is destined to make possible and to protect a society which is exclusively concerned with the materialistic-economic life and its achievements.

WALDEMAR GURIAN

SELECTED BIBLIOGRAPHY

HOBBES, Thomas, *Leviathan,* with an Introduction by Michael Oakeshott. Macmillan.
HOBBES, THOMAS, *Leviathan,* with an Introduction by A. D. Lindsay. Dutton (Everyman's Library).
STRAUSS, Leo, *The Political Philosophy of Hobbes.* Oxford.
GOOCH, G. P., *Proceedings of the British Academy,* Vol. 25. London.
HOBBES, Thomas, *Leviathan,* Book I. Regnery.

Milton: Areopagitica

ON JUNE 14, 1643, the Puritan Parliament of England adopted an ordinance for licensing all books before publication. This act, says Professor Hanford (*A Milton Handbook*, p. 87), "reflected the increasing determination of the Presbyterian party, now in control of Parliament, to reduce English religious practice and opinion to a new uniformity and to silence political opposition." Milton and other men of kindred spirit saw in this ordinance a revival of Stuart tyranny, in particular of a decree of the court of Star Chamber issued in 1637. Milton had enjoyed the three years of freedom created by the abolition of the older decree in 1640, but one of his own writings during this time, *The Doctrine and Discipline of Divorce,* had fallen afoul of the newly imposed censorship. In 1644 he sat down and penned his impassioned defense of the freedom of unlicensed printing. The *Areopagitica* is acknowledgedly his greatest and most eloquent prose work.

Addressed to the Parliament, it is in the form of a classical oration, the title itself coming from Isocrates' speech to the Athenian Court of the Areopagus (in 1624 the French Protestant scholar Jean de Meurs had used the title for a book, *Areopagus, or on the Areopagitic Senate*). It begins with an appeal to the Parliament's "love of truth and uprightness of judgment," to reconsider the act of June 14, 1643. It then outlines the three main arguments to be developed: 1) that the inventors of censorship are "those whom ye will be loath to own"; 2) that the act in question will not realize its intended purpose; 3) that it will discourage all learning and "stop the truth, not only by disexercising and blunting our abilities in what we already know, but by hindering and cropping the discovery that might be yet further made, both in religious and civil wisdom."

Let us consider Milton's arguments and attempt an evaluation of them.

1. Milton declares the inventors of censorship to have been the Council of Trent united with the Spanish Inquisition, which he calls, respectively, "the most anti-christian council, and the most tyrannous inquisition that ever inquired." Yet pagan societies had already practiced censorship. Milton himself points out that in ancient Athens blasphemous and libelous books were forbidden by the magistrate, and that the same thing was done in ancient Rome. The early Christian councils and bishops, says Milton, "were wont only to declare what books were not commendable, passing no further, but leaving it to each one's conscience to read or lay by." As a matter of fact, to cite George H. Putnam (*The Censorship of the Church of Rome*, 1906, I, 1), "Church censorship may be said to have begun as early as 150, with an edict issued by the Council of Ephesus, in which the *Acta Pauli* (an unauthenticated history of the life of St. Paul) was condemned and prohibited." The *Thalia* of Arius was prohibited by the Council of Nice (325), and in 398 a council of Carthage issued a prohibition of Gentile books. The earliest example of a catalog of forbidden books is to be found in the decree of the council held under Pope Gelasius in 494. This is often referred to as the first example of an ecclesiastical *Index*. There are other examples in the centuries before Trent. Naturally the earlier councils could not forbid printing, since printing, as far as Europe was concerned, had not yet been invented.

Milton couples the decrees of Rome and those of the Spanish Inquisition. It should be remarked, however, that these two were separate, and indeed often opposed, organizations. The coalition of Church and State in Spain produced a unique situation, and though for several centuries the Inquisition practiced cruel and severe censorship, Spain "proved the least willing to recognize, in the matter of censorship, the authority of Rome" (Putnam, II, 95). Even the formal *Index* compiled by the Council of Trent and revised and added to ever since, which was the first to have behind it the authority of a general council, was not accepted by Spain (see Putnam, I, 194).

2. That censorship will not perform its intended purpose, Milton demonstrates to his own satisfaction by appealing to the principle of free choice that underlies the practice of virtue. We here come to the heart of Milton's rather Pelagian view of man. His most eloquent passages occur in this section of the speech

(for such it is). "To the pure all things are pure." Books are like viands: "Wholesome meats to a vitiated stomach differ little or nothing from unwholesome; and best books to a naughty mind are not unapplicable to occasions of evil." Temperance is a great virtue, "yet God commits the managing so great a trust, without particular law or prescription, wholly to the demeanor of every grown man." Good and evil grow up together in this world almost inseparably. "He that can apprehend and consider vice with all her baits and seeming pleasures, and yet abstain, and yet distinguish, and yet prefer that which is truly better, he is the true wayfaring Christian."

Noble words! And yet we pray, in a prayer surely used by Milton too: "Lead us not into temptation." Is not Milton too optimistic about human nature? Does he not forget that, if we are the inheritors of Adam's knowledge of good and evil, "that is to say, of knowing good by evil," we are at the same time the inheritors also of that darkening of intellect and enfeeblement of will which followed thereupon? Is man strong enough to resist the temptations he does not avoid? The famous passage that follows contains the contradiction explicitly:

I cannot praise a fugitive and cloistered virtue unexercised and unbreathed, that never sallies out and seeks her adversary, but slinks out of the race, where that immortal garland is to be run for, not without dust and heat. Assuredly we bring not innocence into the world, we bring impurity much rather; that which purifies us is trial, and trial is by what is contrary.

If we bring impurity into the world, does not that mean that we bring weakness and inclination to evil? And can we overcome weakness by subjecting ourselves to occasions of evil? Does it not take greater virtue to resist the temptation to encounter temptation than to welcome temptation in order to test our strength, which is really weakness? The reasoning is perhaps not so illogical as it appears, for Milton was speaking in behalf of an élite of disciplined cultural leaders, yet even here he reveals himself as "a political Utopian" (James H. Hanford, *John Milton, Englishman*, N. Y., 1949, 122). Professor Alfred N. Whitehead even questions whether "the example of Milton's life does not do as much to retard his cause as to advance it" (*Adventures in Ideas*, cited by Merritt Y. Hughes in his Introduction to *Milton: Prose Selections*, N. Y., 1947, lxxxvii).

Milton seems on surer ground when he points out a) that all human learning and controversy can contain hidden dangers to faith and morals, and that it is teachers rather than books that propagate evil doctrines; b) that licensers themselves are not incorruptible; c) that since a wise man can "gather gold out of the drossiest volume," and a fool "will be a fool with the best book, yea or without a book," that is no reason for depriving a wise man of any advantage to his wisdom, "while we seek to restrain from a fool that which being restrained will be no hindrance to his folly."

There is, however, a dubious element in his contention that "if we think to regulate printing, thereby to rectify manners, we must regulate all recreations and pastimes, all that is delightful to man"—singing, dancing, drinking, and even eating. Books appeal directly to mind and will through the symbolism of words. Recreative and sumptuary pleasures only indirectly affect the mind; when carried to excess they are of course vicious. The civil law recognizes their antisocial nature when they incite to riot or delinquency, and punishes the malefactors.

The difficulties and perils of censorship Milton describes well, and we are forced to agree with what he says about the practical impossibility of calling in all old books containing error or immorality, and with his opinion that carefully to examine all new books would require an army of censors, that is to say, expert judges—and where would such an army be found? If there were many books in Milton's day, what about our own, when the presses are turning out books much faster than an army of men can even read them?

3. Milton's final argument against censorship is from the harm it would do if it could be enforced. It would be "the greatest discouragement and affront that can be offered to learning and to learned men." What advantage is it to be a man rather than a boy at school "if we have only escaped the ferula, to come under the fescue of an imprimatur?" He who is not to be trusted with his own actions, especially if he is supposed to be a scholar, is a fool. Certainly a real scholar knows more about what he is writing than some censor perhaps much his inferior in age and judgment. And how can a man teach with authority, which is the life of teaching, when all he teaches "is but under the tuition, under the correction of his patriarchal licenser to blot or alter what precisely accords

not with the hide-bound humour which he calls his judgment?" This act is a slander on the English nation, both governors and governed:

> If it be desired to know the immediate cause of all this free writing and free speaking, there cannot be assigned a truer than your own mild, and free, and human government; it is the liberty, lords and commons, which your own valorous and happy counsels have purchased us. . . . You cannot make us now less capable, less knowing, less eagerly pursuing of the truth, unless ye first make yourselves, that made us so, less the lovers, less the founders of true liberty.

The whole of this impassioned peroration must be read to be felt at its intensest best. The oration closes with Milton's profession of confidence in the ultimate victory of truth in the conflict with error, and a plea for tolerance.

And here it must be noted that at the very end of his long discourse, in an almost casual aside, Milton takes back some of his liberalism. Since all cannot be of one mind, he says, "this doubtless is more wholesome, more prudent, and more Christian, that many be tolerated rather than all compelled." But he at once continues: "I mean not tolerated popery, and open superstition . . . : that also which is impious or evil absolutely either against faith or manners, no law can permit, that intends not to unlaw itself." Does this not sound as if Milton would be the censor, and draw up his own *Index?*

Censorship is a very living problem today, both as regards public morality and the national safety, the latter threatened by totalitarian ideologies. We in the United States consider freedom of speech and of the press one of the basic freedoms of free men, and we have, of course, in the First Amendment to our Constitution, the guarantee that "Congress shall make no law . . . abridging the freedom of speech, or of the press." And yet at this very moment we feel the need of protecting our youth against sensational and pornographic literature (consider the current concern over "comics") and all our people against the poison of subversive political propaganda. No State could endure, no religion could remain intact, which tolerated all manner of opinions and doctrines. Even advocates of liberty as intransigent as Milton admit that. Liberty of conscience and of thought (in the sense of opinion) is not in question here. Liberty to utter opinion is. It pertains to civil and ecclesiastical authority to limit the latter in certain circumstances, in behalf of the common good, the one by civil, the other by spiritual means.

Ecclesiastical censorship, both preventive and punitive, is no longer, in free societies, coupled with civil; it applies no suasions but moral ones, and no sanctions but spiritual ones. Where all are of the same faith, the State may act against heretics and their writings as endangering the common good. Where, as in the United States, doctrinal unity is lacking, the State must still protect itself against the subversion of its social and political foundations (e.g., if certain groups should advocate polygamy or the overthrow of the government), but must leave a wide margin of tolerance; in this area religious authority may exercise its moral and spiritual control. The ecclesiastical proscription of books and articles dangerous to faith and morals is, when rightly undertaken, nothing but a means of saving men from falling into spiritual morasses. No one would object to signs prohibiting trespass where a bridge has collapsed or mines have been planted, on the ground that this would be an infringement of liberty or an obstacle to the development of physical strength and courage. Similarly, reasons the ecclesiastical censor, there are enough positive ways of developing virtue and knowledge without deliberately inviting added risks in the form of immoral and irreligious books. Indeed, the whole purpose of the *Index* is to help the faithful. It was impossible for the Church, says Hilgers (*Der Index der Verbotenen Buecher,* 1904), without neglecting its duty, to avoid the responsibility of supervising the literary production and reading of the faithful. The theory of ecclesiastical censorship is thus intelligible, though it may, of course, be abused or maladministered.

As regards civil censorship, even our free society, it seems, cannot do entirely without it. The postmaster general can deny second class mailing privileges to publications containing matter forbidden by certain Federal statutes. The national government, under the interstate commerce power, has forbidden the importation or transportation of obscene and brutalizing films. The motion-picture producers have set up a voluntary self-censorship, and certain municipalities control the exhibition of motion pictures through police power. The radio broadcasting stations are prohibited, by the Federal Communications Commission, from using profane or obscene language or denying equal rights to legal candidates for public office. Though the theatre has never been subjected to formal censorship in the United States, there has been much local control by the police. The distribution of books has been interfered with by the postal law, the customs law, and local ordinances and self-appointed groups, the latter sometimes very Puritanical.

Our constitutional guarantees of freedom of speech and the press cannot be too jealously guarded. In the past there have been violations of its spirit (especially during war-time, perhaps never more than during World War I), and there may be again. If the principles which ought to guide any defensible censorship are difficult to state, they are even more difficult to administer. Prudence and tolerance must join with zeal for the public good, as Milton reminds us in unforgettable phrases, for,

unless wariness be used, as good almost kill a man as kill a good book: who kills a man kills a reasonable creature, God's image; but he who destroys a good book, kills reason itself, kills the image of God, as it were, in the eye. Many a man lives a burden to the earth; but a good book is the precious life-blood of a master-spirit, embalmed and treasured up on purpose to a life beyond life.

VICTOR M. HAMM

SELECTED BIBLIOGRAPHY

HANFORD, J. H., *A Milton Handbook*. Crofts.
HANFORD, J. H., *John Milton, Englishman*. Crown.
HILGERS, J., *Der Index der Verbotenen Buecher*. Freiburg.
HUGHES, M. Y. (Ed.), *Milton: Prose Selections*. Odyssey.
PATTERSON, F. A. (Ed.), *The Student's Milton*. Crofts.
PUTNAM, G. H., *The Censorship of the Church of Rome*. Putnam.
WHIPPLE, LEON, *The Story of Civil Liberty in the United States*. Vanguard.
MILTON, JOHN, *Areopagitica*. Regnery.

Swift: Gulliver's Travels

FROM THE DAY it was published, the *Travels into Several Remote Nations of the World* of Lemuel Gulliver was known for a great book. Captain Gulliver walked easily and with gigantic stride into that select company of figures of literature who are not only triumphantly themselves but who take on the habiliments of national and world myth. So it was from the first; so it is—despite all that has happened in the world since 1726—today. Prince Posterity, upon whom the author long had a cautious eye, still pays this book the compliment of the "shock of recognition." When Gulliver peers down at the inhabitants of the diminutive kingdom of Lilliput, he gazes upon us. We are vicariously Gulliver as he discovers in the Utopian land of the giants a standard with which to compare our governments, laws and wars. Our own time is even more prolific of projectors, scientific and political, than ever the eighteenth century was. Of course, as Thackeray said of literary snobs, there are no modern Yahoos.

The book was sold out in its first week, and a tumult of editions and imitators has followed down to our own day. Gulliver was read delightedly in the royal chamber and in the more than royal boudoir of Sarah, Duchess of Marlborough. The wits were ecstatic. Pope journeyed from Twickenham to London to observe Gulliver's effect on society. A hit, a palpable hit! was the consensus, Although the book was written more to vex than divert, all were diverted, even those who saw themselves broadly hinted at. After all, the raps were generously distributed, for Swift had acted on the Irish tradition of hitting a head wherever you see one, and who would not prefer being Swift's Flimnap to Pope's Sporus? Few there were who were so dismayed by the book's "improbable lies" as not to believe a word of it!

Swift's contemporaries anticipated posterity's verdict to an astonishing degree. *Gulliver* was immediately seen to be of the

stature and command of Bunyan's *Pilgrim's Progress,* and as long
a life was prophesied for it. The comparison was a felicitous one,
for Lemuel Gulliver takes his place beside Christian as one of
three symbolic figures of the age. The third figure is, of course,
Robinson Crusoe. Each provides an aspect of Everyman as the
age saw him. Christian is Everyman as evangelical, entering no
less into secular triumph than into the Heavenly City. Despite
the hardships he encounters, Crusoe is Everyman at his slippered
ease, secularized to a calm acceptance of creature comforts and
quite capable of supplying most of them himself. There is a
return to evangelism in Gulliver, for all his rationalist spirit;
Everyman, if he can no longer occupy himself with seeking the
Heavenly City, can at least hurl Jeremiads at the earthly one. In
a composite of the three the middle class could see its own temper
and its image.

Thomas Wolfe, for whom the Gulliver image held special
poignance, considered *Gulliver's Travels* one of the most autobiographical books ever written. If *Gulliver* is autobiography, it
is inverted autobiography, as is everything Swift wrote, for inversion is the key to his technique, from larger forms down to individual sentences. In the proud obverse of the "little language" to
Stella, Swift wrote in these pages in big, formal language the life
story of his mind. But the book is metaphor, not outline. It is
worse than fatuous to expect to find, say, in Gulliver's wry appreciation of the title *nardac* conferred upon him by the emperor of
Lilliput, Swift's own displeasure in the mitreless title of dean
reluctantly permitted him by Queen Anne. Yet the mind of
Gulliver becomes the mind of Swift. At first Gulliver is a straw
man, a *naïf* for whom king and country are adequate shibboleth,
with Swift just off stage pulling the strings. Then, as the book
nears its frightening conclusion, Swift and Gulliver are one. And
the rest is Yahoo.

Both had experience of power and of helplessness. Swift was
born with much of the talent but little of the opportunity of
command. He was doomed to a lifetime of little empire and of
imperious sway over kingdoms he despised. Only fitfully did he
assume the artist's sceptre to find, in symbol and allegory, empire
more lasting than that Harley ruled. Like Anna in Pope's *Rape
of the Lock,* he "did sometimes counsel take, and sometimes tea."
All the relations of his life he considered in terms of command.

In his latter years, thinking back on the days when he was the confidant of ministers of state, he was bitterly aware that he was "acting the same things in miniature." "My realm," he wrote, "extends a hundred and twenty houses, whose inhabitants constitute the bulk of my subjects." He walked abroad in his wig and gown, or rode his horse, sometimes forty miles a day, like a giant among pygmies. After Stella's death he dined alone—"like a king" is his word for it. As dean of St. Patrick's he held his archbishop at bay and his chapter in thralldom.

It all began early enough. Posthumous son of an impoverished father and of a race that had suffered for its loyalty to the Stuarts, he passed through his early education and his days at Trinity a stranger to his surroundings. Pride and superior scorn were native to him. His secretaryship to Sir William Temple, a great diplomat and a great gentleman, provided him the material for a life in "the pride of literature," then becoming a sovereign republic. But he always seems to have felt that at Moor Park he was seated below the salt. When somewhat later he represented the cause of the Church of Ireland (and the cause of Jonathan Swift) in London, he summoned; he exhorted; he gave commands. "With Princes kept a due Decorum, But never stood in Awe before 'em," he slanged in doggerel.

When he dined, the company would be limited at his orders, and dukes might seek entrée in vain. At Twickenham he would plan the lives of Pope, his host, and their friend John Gay for three or four days together. In one of the many anecdotes associated with his name it is reported that the people left off trampling his hedges, where they had gathered to see an eclipse, and went to their homes upon the word that the phenomenon had been postponed by order of the dean! When events proved stubborn, friends were at hand for bullying. Worthy of his steel were Stella, the serene yet iron-willed pupil of his youth down through the middle years, and Vanessa, who flung herself at him, to be rebuffed by his cold, insuperable will. Negligently and with his rapier pen he ruled Ireland. The passion for command, extended more rigorously to friend than foe, caused him to dictate in anticipation the reaction to his death:

> Poor Pope will grieve a Month; and Gay
> A Week; and Arbuthnot a Day.

His arm of power extended beyond his death—in his stony epitaph for all to read of the savage indignation now at rest, and in the Swift Hospital, existing in Dublin to this day, which he left by will to the mad.

He was like Gulliver in this: an actor on a stage most infamously crowded, he seemed a spectator. Swift was what Shaw claimed for himself—up to the neck in the life of his time—yet he was always looking over his shoulder at something else. He walked, the observer, in a world he never made. A clergyman who acted like a soldier (and who reminded his bishop he was not to be treated as a footman); a wit who was a statesman; a man whose rage and resentment made him the "patriot" he did not seek to be; a fierce hater whose constant cry was the dilettante's *vive la bagatelle*—he was all and none of these things. Ireland was his Lilliput, and England the Flying Island poised menacingly over his head. Much of the book assuredly can be received as conscious allegory; Swift-Gulliver is, as was the dean, alternately impotent and raging. Yet the most striking "autobiographical" passages in *Gulliver* are those untouched by his design—life is forever imitating this book—such as the passage on the unhappy, immortal Struldbruggs which foretells Swift's last years of madness and neglect.

If this book is a life of Swift, it is also, or has been taken to be, a "life" of his times. Without Harley and Bolingbroke, without the ever-hated Walpole, without the dumpy queen who thwarted him of a mitre, without the friends he bullied, without John Churchill, Duke of Marlborough, to personify for him both war and plunder, the book would not be. All this is true; this book is, but only among other things, a "politico-sociological treatise." To make too much of the contemporary irritants which provided Swift-Gulliver with his *exemplum* is almost to argue that had Swift been born out of his proper time there would have been no conniving politicians, no liars, no cheats, no "mankind" for him to write about. "Fools are my theme," sang Byron, "let satire be my song." Fools are a recurrent crop, and except that our own day might be said to have out-Yahooed the tribe Swift knew, his satire would find in any age its home, and its victims in any land their habitat.

The Age of Queen Anne provided the matter; from Swift alone, from his lifetime of devotion to style (the right words in the right places, according to his definition) came the form. In the form—great literature's only true originality—is the book's triumph. Because of it the book belongs to literature first of all, and only secondarily to politics and sociology. What *Gulliver* might have been had not form prevailed we know from Part III, the least successful part, as Dr. Arbothnot frankly told the author. Here Gulliver is the completely disembodied spectator of a series of fads and fancies, of mathematical speculators, of professors of political science, of a kind of television in reverse, which brings forth a pageant from the past to contrast its worthies with the fawning imposters of the present. Here is the sort of thing Pope could have done and pretty much did in his *Art of Sinking in Poetry*. Here is the *improvisatore* at work, tossing off choice bits amid much dullness. But the rest of the book, particularly the brilliant first half, is fable in Aristotle's sense. It is that successful kind of fable that elicits the wonder of childhood the while it keeps old men from the chimney corner. Dr. Johnson was never wider of the mark than when he said: "When once you have thought of big men and little men, it is very easy to do all the rest."

After all, Swift was not the first to think of these things, and we shall probably never know what all his sources were. What hints Lucian, Rabelais, and De Bergerac supplied, we can never surely say. The *Voyages et avantes de Jaqques Masse* seems very like, and Gildon's *Fortunate Shipwreck* may have provided a hint or two (as may the despised Defoe), but their likenesses only go to prove how far from model Swift was in this and everything he wrote. "What porridge ate John Keats?" jests Browning; the question is always a footless one. For Leigh Hunt, no scholar, but one who both knew and loved literature, it was enough that, though Swift rethought his predecessors' thoughts, "they ended in results quite masterly, and his own." On this matter let Dr. Johnson have the last word. "The pursuer of Swift," he says in that curious masterpiece, the *Lives of the Poets*, "wants little previous knowledge; it will be sufficient that he is acquainted with common words and common things."

From the common knowledge of life the reader can enter into this most self-contained, and in some ways most magical, of all the imagined worlds of literature. With great matter-of-factness Gulliver sketches the background of his early life and education in the opening pages and recounts briefly and with casual realism his two early sets of voyages. On his next voyage, after a storm which drives the ship near Tasmania, the vessel founders on a rock. Gulliver swims until he can feel bottom, then walks to the shore, where he falls asleep. He awakes to find himself fastened to the ground, and he feels something on his left leg. "Bending my eyes downward as much as I could," he relates, "I perceived it to be a human creature not six inches high, with bow and arrow in his hands, and a quiver at his back."

At these words we enter the novelist's realm, scarcely to become aware of the real world until Gulliver returns from his final voyage. Everything is drawn to scale: the houses, the trees, the livestock. Nor is this proportion forgotten in relation to Gulliver; the Lilliputians see the contents of Gulliver's pockets (in a passage Dr. Johnson grudgingly admired) according to their scale of physical and mental vision. Realism and satire combine, as in Swift-Gulliver's description of the emperor. "He is taller, by almost the breadth of my nail, than any in his court"—and then the tail-sting—"which alone is enough to strike an awe into the beholders." Many are the sly digs in Part I, by satire of likes and contraries, on "the nature of ministers and princes." A powerful, ironic fusion of the literal and figurative (a trick used so devastatingly in the *Modest Proposal*) occurs often, as when a friend at court tells Gulliver his eyes are to be put out as punishment for his treasonable intentions and points out that "it would be sufficient for you to see by the eyes of the ministers, since the greatest princes do no more."

Swift provides us with no obvious system for interpreting his work, but we may conveniently take *Gulliver's Travels* as a study in relativity. The physically relative is explored in the first two adventures. Part III exploits intellectual relativity, to deliver a characteristically British judgment on the relative value of the speculative and the practical. In the savage final travel the moral judgments previously expressed are heightened to show the relative morality of men and horses. Here Swift finds Aristotle's definition of the rational animal realized in the horse, rather than in the degenerate Yahoo-man, a thing of filth. At last, after the false Utopia of Brobdingnag, for giants are only men writ large, we come to the true rational republic. (Should anything be made of the fact that the three other lands Gulliver visits are kingdoms, and the country of the Houyhnhnms alone is a republic?)

Swift the realist and contributor to the form of the novel is seen to best advantage in the land of the giants. Like Redcrosse, Gulliver encounters "An hideous Geant horrible and hye," yet here is no land of faery, but sober fact. This part of the book is, in every sense, on more generous lines than the one preceding. Here is the one character (other than Gulliver) drawn at any length. She is the hardened voyager's nine-year-old nurse, a creature "very good natured, and not above forty foot high, being little for her age." The satire too is generously proportioned and removed from pettiness; human grandeur is mimicked even more when *homunculus Europeaus* looks up at human creatures of upwards of sixty feet than when he declines his eyes to gaze upon men six inches high.

"I dare engage," says the king of Brobdingnag, a more thoughtful Gargantua than ever Rabelais knew, "these creatures have their titles and distinctions of honor, they contrive little burrows, that they call houses and cities; they make a figure in dress and equipage; they love, they fight, they dispute, they betray." The horrified narrator rises to this bait, for Swift has not yet permitted the iron to enter Gulliver's soul. He bounces back from the king's description of Englishmen as a "most pernicious race of little odious vermin" to offer the astounded monarch, a victim of "confined education" and "short views," the formula for gunpowder, which is sternly rejected. Gulliver learns more of this admirable country, and of its simply written laws, to discover a Utopia where "to write a comment upon any law is a capital crime." And it is the former unsuccessful Trinity student who received a "bad" in philosophy and a "negligent" in theology who writes: "And as to ideas, entities, abstractions and transcendentals, I could never drive the least conception into their heads."

The high humor of the book derives from the happy fact that Gulliver is as prosaic and unimaginative as Crusoe. In fact, in not one of Gulliver's difficulties, when his eyeballs are at the mercy of the Lilliputian bowmen or when he is attacked by a gigantic monkey (the size of an elephant), does he become as excited as Crusoe does over the mere discovery of a footprint. Gulliver's experiences "contain little besides common events," yet he justly observes that his account of the Struldbruggs, those unhappy immortals who decline by harshly perceptible degrees and who cannot even hold a conversation after they become two hundred, is "a little out of the common way."

In the fourth and final of the unfortunate voyages quiet realism and sober recording once again come to the traveler's assistance. The surgeon turned sea captain again comes ashore in a perfectly natural way, this time through mutiny in his crew. In a very short time he has learned to hate the loathsome Yahoos, who parody mankind, and to reverence the rational horses. Swift and Gulliver are one at last; the latter will be gulled no more. The mask is off, and Europe has become as pestilential to Gulliver as it has been all along to his creator. Law, money, commerce, diplomacy, war—for none of these things has a Houyhnhnm language.

But Gulliver's felicity—life without "lords, fiddlers, judges or dancing masters"—does not last. He is "exhorted" (so mild is the rule of reason) out of the country. The manner of his going provides a remarkable and yet typical passage. "I took," he tells us, "a second leave of my master: but as I was going to prostrate myself to kiss his hoof, he did me the honor to raise it gently to my mouth." And then the superb *riposte*: "I am not ignorant how much I have been censured for mentioning this last particular. For my detractors are pleased to think it improbable, that so illustrious a person should descend to give so great a mark of distinction to a creature so inferior as I." Notice what happens under Swift's control; what an unexpected consequence follows the word "improbable." The key to much of Swift's art is contained in this brief passage.

It is often forgotten that Swift, satire apart, was a humorist, one of our greatest. Were mankind always under his lash there would be no delight to be found in the book other than that promoted by the flaying of folly. The humor in *Gulliver* is often overlooked because it is that mirth without laughter which the age demanded. "In my mind," says Lord Chesterfield, "there is nothing so illiberal, and so ill-bred, as audible laughter." True wit, he holds, will do no more than "give a cheerfulness to the countenance." We must not expect to find in *Gulliver* humor of the visceral type. If we are content with verbal sleight of hand

and the inaudible laughter of the mind, we shall discover, with Dr. Arbuthnot, that this is a "merry book."

Yet it remains to be said that in *Gulliver's Travels* there are passages one might wish had been blotted, that the notes of serenity and repose proper to true breadth and greatness of spirit are lacking here. Thackeray would no more have admitted Swift to his drawing room than he would an ancient Briton, yet eighteenth-century manners alone do not explain those passages which Aldous Huxley credits to Swift's hatred of the "poor, harmless, necessary tripes." Swift was a squeamish man, and on occasion one of nasty ideas. But he was above prurience and innuendo. Nor did his "system of misanthropy," like Timon's, offer mankind a halter. He was the Savonarola of pamphleteering; an honest reformer, however unpleasant a one. Although he jested that he expected his readers to reform completely in six months (just as all faults in conversation could be corrected in half an hour), there was no jest in his claim to having written to instruct and inform:

> His Satyr points at no Defect
> But what all Mortals may correct.

He could not himself attain the condition of happiness, the state of being a fool among knaves, and he suffered greatly for it. He paid, as Savonarola paid, for being a perfectionist. But his pride was humbled; in the last terrible years he knew at length what he was.

Gulliver's Travels is his monument; as long as books last, this one will. Human folly is such that today's events, and tomorrow's, will seem a most particular gloss of this book's extravagances. A chief product of the Age of Reason, as England knew it, this book destroyed the cautious structure reflected by Pope's *Essay on Man*. It announces the failure of the neoclassical spirit and ushers in the Romantic Age. This lasting book provides us with one of the great recurring truths of (to transpose Newman's words a bit) our sinful literature of sinful man: the wandering Adam, the observer and the witness. Lemuel Gulliver fills no inconsiderable place in the five centuries of witness from Piers to Melville's Ishmael. He has raised great questions which we have yet to answer.

RILEY HUGHES

SELECTED BIBLIOGRAPHY

CASE, Arthur E., *Four Essays on Gulliver's Travels*. Princeton University.
DAVIS, Herbert, *The Satire of Jonathan Swift*. Macmillan.
EDDY, William A., *Gulliver's Travels: A Critical Study*. Princeton University.
GWYNN, Stephen, *The Life and Friendships of Dean Swift*. Holt.
TAYLOR, W. D., *Jonathan Swift: A Critical Essay*. London: Davies.
VAN DOREN, Carl (Ed.), *The Portable Swift*. Viking.
VAN DOREN, Carl, *Swift*. Viking.
SWIFT, Jonathan, *Gulliver's Travels*. Random (Modern Library).
SWIFT, Jonathan, *Gulliver's Travels*. Dutton (Everyman's Library).
SWIFT, Jonathan, *Gulliver's Travels*, Books I and II. Regnery.

Pascal: Pensées

WHEN PASCAL died at the age of thirty-nine in 1662, his family found a great number of notes written on pieces of paper varying in size from a full page to a mere scrap. Some were long, well-developed analyses and demonstrations, while others were short paragraphs, individual sentences, or even just a few words which are frequently meaningless to us as we read them out of their context, but which were doubtless sufficient to recall a whole train of thought to their author.

No one was surprised to find these papers, for it had been long known that Pascal was preparing an "Apology" of the Christian religion, and it was awaited with the greatest eagerness by his friends. Such an "Apology," or demonstration of the truth of the Christian religion, written by such a man, could not but be of the very highest interest and value. Pascal's extraordinary intellectual gifts had been manifest from his childhood; his father, a highly respected jurist and scientist, had felt obliged to steer his precocious young son away from mathematics at a very early age for fear he would neglect the study of languages. He is nonetheless reported to have discovered the first thirty-two theorems of Euclid for himself by the age of twelve. At seventeen, he published an essay on conic sections and at about that time also invented his *machine arithmétique.* His pathfinding work in mathematics and physics is well known to scholars in those fields and is sufficient to establish his stature as an outstanding figure in the history of science.

He was, then, widely known to excel in what he called the *esprit de géométrie,* by which he meant not only the spirit of geometry, but that of all precise, "scientific" reasoning and demonstration. His reputation for the most scrupulous and critical regard for fact and the justifiable implications of fact, and his rejection of a-prioristic reasoning on insufficient bases was above suspicion. How sound and how cogent must be an "Apology of the Christian Religion" coming from such a man, who had devoted years of his best effort and deepest interest to it! How impossible for the unbelievers to dismiss it, as they did so many others, as the work of superstition, ignorance, folly or stupidity!

What is at least equally important is that he was known to excel not only in this *esprit de géométrie* but also in what he opposed to it, the *esprit de finesse*. This latter is much more difficult to define. By it, he meant the ability to discern intuitively what is true, good or fine without recourse to discursive reason. The processes of this spirit are quite different from those of "geometry." It proceeds quickly and directly to its object, which usually lies in the field of more common human experience than the object of speculative reason. It is closer to our modern idea of "judgment," or, in the field of the arts, of "taste." It enables us to be successful in the conduct of our personal and social lives, rather than in the pursuit of scientific truth. It enables us to understand our neighbor and to make our thoughts understandable to him.

Pascal remarked that those endowed with the *esprit de géométrie* were very seldom gifted with the *esprit de finesse,* and vice versa. His friends, however, know very well that he was superbly favored in both respects. They had had a convincing demonstration of this fact in a conference he was prevailed upon to deliver to a group of them some three or four years before his death, in which he outlined to them his projected "Apology" in a session that lasted almost three hours. It held them spellbound, and they emerged from it more eager than ever to see the finished work.

As his sister, Madame Périer, wrote in her Life of her brother, however, God disposes, and the work was never finished. We have only these fragmentary notes, not all of which were intended for the "Apology," and in no particular order. Very soon after his death these fragments were pasted in large albums, again in no particular order, or rather in an order dictated by the size and shape of the paper the fragments were written on, so as to form a mosaic pasted onto the pages of the album. This haphazard arrangement has of course caused his modern editors great difficulty in their efforts to sort out the fragments and put them

into an acceptable order. In this task they are aided by the somewhat contradictory accounts which have come down to us of the
outline Pascal himself indicated in his famous conference referred to above.

Still, in this extremely fragmentary and unordered collection,
mankind has recognized one of its very greatest books, one in
which a human mind and spirit of tremendous power and depth
speaks to us eloquently and forcefully of what is most important
to us in the world, namely, ourselves and our destiny. For Pascal
realized the impossibility of coercing the mind of the unbeliever
to accept Christian truth by the power of pure logical reasoning
alone. True faith is, of course, a gift from the hands of God,
which no man can obtain by his own efforts, much less have
forced upon him by another man's arguments, however sound
they may be. All that the apologist can do is to try to serve, so
far as his inspiration and gifts allow, as an instrument in presenting the truth to the unbeliever in such a manner as to remove
obstacles to its acceptance and to inspire the wish to receive it.
When man truly and humbly seeks for the truth, we must confidently hope that it will not be denied to him: "You would not
seek Me, if you had not already found Me."

Pascal's greatest originality lies in his insight into human
nature, its ingenious and devious workings in its flight from
reality and truth, and in his extraordinary ability to bring us up
short in this flight and make us take thought. For the first obstacle to the acceptance of truth is our dislike of thinking seriously about the basic things of our human existence: what we
are, why we are, even where we are. These thoughts disturb and
frighten us, and we avoid them like the plague. Pascal himself,
with his ardent faith, felt more than awe when looking into the
vastnesses surrounding us: *Le silence de ces espaces infinis
m'effraie* ("The silence of this infinite space strikes me with
fear.") And so it would all of us, particularly the unbeliever,
if we ever really allowed ourselves to think seriously about it.

Pitilessly, irrefutably, Pascal shows us the shoddiness of our
multiple devices for shielding ourselves from these unwelcome
proddings, not so much of our consciences as of our sense and
our senses. First of all, we seek refuge in human society and
diversion. Hence the distress we feel in prolonged solitude, and
hence also our eternal need of distraction and entertainment.

Pascal's picture of our state of mind is so timelessly true that we seem to hear him remind us that hence comes our *need* of the movies, the radio, the comics, the bars, the parties, the television, not so much as a flight from the problems and anxieties of our day, the political and social unrest, as from our own individual intellectual, moral and spiritual dissatisfaction with ourselves. And so it was in Pascal's day; merely the mode of distraction was different.

All this Pascal knew from personal experience, from his years of "worldly" life, when, although he apparently never lost the Faith, he frequented the fashionable work of French "libertine" society. The term then meant something closer to our "free-thinker" than to the English word "libertine," although the *libertins* of the seventeenth century were not only atheists or agnostics but were frequently also given to gambling, debauchery and loose living. Pascal, then, knew this world intimately, had many friends who belonged to it, among them some of brilliant intellect, and perhaps some of basically good intentions.

It is to these last that the "Apology" is principally directed. There doubtless existed then, as now, very many men of good will who hungered after the truth, but who were prevented from obtaining or even seeking it, by the obstacles placed in their way by themselves or others: their love of comfort and pleasure, their fear of effort, their lack of intellectual or religious training or, most dangerous and terrible of all such obstacles, the bad example of some professing and perhaps sincere believers around them. This provides sufficient specious justification for retreating into skepticism, agnosticism and indifference.

It is precisely from this lethargic folly of indifference that Pascal would rouse his unbeliever. In his perfect candor, he admits that the sight of a man in this state irritates him more than it arouses pity. He feels like the man who cannot convince the youngster that it is criminal folly to go skating on the pond that is only very lightly frozen over; when reason and persuasion fail to make any impression, we must be superhuman not to feel irritation at such stubborn folly.

This feeling of false security with which we lull ourselves into indifference is the first obstacle in the way of our acceptance of the Faith, and it is therefore Pascal's first target in his campaign against his libertine's smug complacency. He shows us our frail humanity precariously perched between two terrifying and unknown infinities, that of the infinitely great, the enormous, unfathomable and eternally mysterious astronomical space, lost in the midst of which man is a mere tiny fleck, and, on the other hand, the infinity of the infinitestimally small, that microscopic world that was just beginning to be suspected and explored in Pascal's day. Each minutest particle of matter so considered becomes a universe in itself, and presumably each such universe is infinitely divisible into tinier and tinier particles, beyond the stretch of human reason and imagination. We must really be unusually benumbed in our habits of thoughtlessness or vice if such considerations do not succeed in arousing in us some sense of giddiness as we teeter on our little perch surrounded by infinities of boundless magnitudes of space on the one hand and by endless infinities of tiny universes within and beneath us. On this purely natural plane of the libertine and the atheist, what an appalling, senseless lot is human existence, no more significant or valuable than that of the invisibly microscopic creature we crush when we set a glass down on a table.

But Pascal would not abandon us to this frozen terror. When man has finally realized to some extent his miserable weakness and smallness, not only on the material plane but on the intellectual and moral as well, it is time to point out to him the authentic greatness that is also his. It is true that man is a mere reed, Pascal tells us, but he is a *thinking* reed, and "thinking constitutes his greatness." Here Pascal brings into play his concept, essential in his thinking, of the "order of values." Miserable, weak and helpless in his material existence as man is, he transcends it completely by his mind and his spirit, which are of an entirely different order and are incommensurable with material things. Here we are shown the grandeur of man's rational and creative genius. Man is both miserably weak and spiritually great; both of these contradictory statements are true, but neither one is the whole truth. Taken separately, they will lead us either to utter despair or to the wildest extravagances of pride; taken together they give us a true and balanced view of human nature.

Having thus endeavored first to shake our complacent indifference, and then to teach us to avoid the extremes of despair and pride, Pascal would show us the one religion of all religions that adequately accounts for this curiously dual nature of ours.

No other explains both our greatness and our misery; only the doctrine of the Creation and the Fall of man gives us any adequate account of what each of us finds within himself.

This religion, then, of all religions, is *venerable*. It explains to us what we most need to know and what no other can teach us: what we are and why we are as we are. It is thus, at the very least, entitled to our deep respect. And so another great barrier falls, for then as now, one of the defenses we may erect against belief is the claim that the faith is "backward," "superstitious," suitable only for the ignorant and unthinking.

When indifference and scorn of the Faith have been overcome, when religion is considered with interest and respect, the next obstacle to be overcome is *dislike* of the Faith, reluctance to believe it true, which often stems from fear that it will oblige us to forego the pleasures and the self-indulgence we have enjoyed for so long. We may have to exchange these for repentance and disagreeable self-discipline and self-denial. It is at this point that Pascal's too-famous "wager" is introduced. In it Pascal is a mathematician, almost a statistician, calculating possibilities, chances, weighing advantages against disadvantages in a purely matter-of-fact evaluation of possible and probable profit-and-loss.

Mathematicians, philosophers and many others have written a great deal about this Pascalian "wager," some of them to impugn its validity, others to express distaste for its apparently coldly calculating and purely egotistical approach to religion. Most of those who have criticized the "wager" adversely have made the grave error in method of taking it by itself, out of its context. It is not in any sense the crux of Pascal's apologetic, as some seem to think it; it applies and is intended to apply only at this precise point where our *libertin* skeptic has begun to think seriously about religion and to consider the Faith with respect, but still shies away from it for fear he has more to lose than to gain.

At this point Pascal shows that he cannot avoid the wager: whether he will or not, he must wager. Whether he continue to live or decide to commit suicide, he must either by his disbelief wager in effect that the religion is false or, by his embracing it, wager that it is true. Now this way of looking at religious faith may seem repugnant to many, but it corresponds admirably to the state of mind of Pascal's wavering freethinker at this point of the dialog between him and our author.

Pascal then shows him how little he has to lose: a few miserable self-indulgences that do not by any means give him even human peace and happiness, against a possible gain of infinite good and eternal joy. Even if the chances were only one in favor of the Faith being true against an infinity of its being false, even then human reason and prudence would dictate a choice of the wager that it is true, because of the insignificance of our possible loss against the immeasurable felicity of our possible gain. But the chance is not an infinity against one, but one against one; it is at least as likely that the Faith is true as that it is not. Thus, in a coldly calculating way, it is folly to do otherwise than wager the Faith is true, and wager we must whether we will or no. It is infinitely to our *interest* that it be true; we must profoundly wish it to be true. The Faith is, then, not only worthy of our deepest respect, but also of our fervent love and desire.

From this point on, apparently, Pascal's apologetic would follow a more familiar and traditional line. This is necessarily so, since, having attempted to remove the obstacles we put in the way of an open-minded, honest attempt to assess the reasonableness of belief, we can then more profitably look into the claims of that faith. The deepest truths of religion cannot, of course, be proven by our human reason, but must be accepted on faith.

But that faith is above and beyond reason, not contrary to it. For just as the order of reason and mind is essentially distinct from and higher than that of matter, so the order of charity and grace is equally distinct from and higher than that of reason. Not all the arguments of the greatest minds of the world can by themselves produce one act of charity. One manifestation of God's charity toward His human creatures is the sending of divine Revelation to impart to them essential religious truths which the limited human intellect is incapable of arriving at unaided, more radically incapable than is the mind of a cat to understand the precession of the equinoxes or to build a cathedral.

Hence Pascal will not attempt to "prove" the content of Revelation to the nonbeliever, but he will, following the necessary and traditional method of apologetics at this point, endeavor to establish the historical *fact* of Revelation, of the divine authority of that Revelation. Our rationalistic or skeptical nonbeliever must first be shown that the Faith is not something arbitrarily propounded by Catholics without basis or valid claims to authority. There must be acceptable, disinterested *witness* to its authenticity. That witness was not far to seek in Pascal's day, nor is it today: it is the existence and testimony of the Witness People, the Jewish People, who will play that role until the second coming of Christ at the end of this world. They carry the prophecies which clearly predicted the coming of Christ; they still do so, though they do not recognize the meaning of the prophecies to which they bear witness. Their testimony is, therefore, all the more valuable, since it is totally disinterested.

Here Pascal reviews (and if he had lived, he would undoubtedly have developed this central portion of his demonstration) the prophecies and their realization in the life of Christ and the history of the Church. He shows the central position of the Person of Christ in Revelation: the prophets who prophesied but were not themselves prophesied; the saints who were prophesied, but did not themselves prophesy; Christ alone who both prophesied and was prophesied. His very rejection by God's Chosen People was foretold in the very prophecies to which they themselves bear ununderstanding witness.

The validity of this section of Pascal's work can be judged only by the professional exegete. One of the most eminent authorities in this field, the great Dominican scholar Père Lagrange, has borne eloquent witness (in the *Revue Biblique,* 1906) to the permanent value of Pascal's interpretations of the Bible. This is perhaps the most astounding of all the evidence of Pascal's powers of mind and heart, and no doubt also of divine guidance granted him, since Biblical exegesis was certainly the most undeveloped of ecclesiastical sciences in his day, and he was then treading on very uncertain ground.

When the skeptic has been thus prepared to accept the authority of divine Revelation, to respect and love the religion founded upon it, he has removed the most serious obstacles hitherto blocking the entrance of God's grace into his soul. No train of reasoning, however valid and compelling, will bring faith to him, but it may bring him toward the Faith. If we, believer and nonbeliever, sincerely and humbly seek for God, we must confidently hope that the treasures of His inexhaustible love will not be denied us. We must try to prepare the way, open our reason and our hearts to God and remember the promise that if we ask it will be given us. Then faith and grace can flow into our hearts and we can at last find peace in the presence of God felt in our heart, which is Pascal's final definition of faith: *Dieu sensible au coeur.*

JEAN PAUL MISRAHI

SELECTED BIBLIOGRAPHY

MAURIAC, F., *Living Thoughts of Blaise Pascal.* Longmans, Green.
BREMOND, ABBÉ, *Literary History of Religious Thought in France.* Macmillan.
GIRAUD, V., *Vie héroique de Blaise Pascal.* Paris: Gres.
STROWSKI, F., *Pascal et son temps.* Plon.
PASCAL, Blaise, *Pensées.* Dutton (Everyman's Library).
PASCAL, Blaise, *Pensées.* Regnery.

Rousseau: A Discourse on Political Economy, On the Origin of Inequality

IT IS UNFORTUNATE that, for its study of Rousseau, the Great Books Foundation invited its subscribers to read *The Social Contract* before the *On the Origin of Inequality* and *A Discourse on Political Economy.* *The Social Contract* (1762) is one of Rousseau's last works, while the other two (1754, 1755) were written shortly after the essay that first brought him fame in 1750: *Did the Development of the Sciences and the Arts Contribute to Purify Morals?* The reading of the latter short essay should have been required first, to be followed by the two we are now asked to consider, the whole as preliminary to reading *The Social Contract.*

One reason for the need of studying Rousseau's works chronologically is that Rousseau's thought, despite its latent unity, is, as we saw in our study of *The Social Contract* (see *The Great Books*, Vol. I, pp. 85-91), a tissue of inconsistencies: as Albert Schinz has so well shown in his *La Pensée de J. J. Rousseau*, there were two Rousseaus unreconciled—the romantic, and the Roman and Calvinist; the optimistic sentimentalist, and the Stoic and pessimist. The first yearned to believe in the natural goodness of man, the second was convinced that man was bad and needed discipline.

Brought up by an artisan Genevan father, encouraged to do some high thinking on his own, Rousseau early read Plutarch, Tacitus and Grotius. But he also read the sentimental novels of the early seventeenth century: D'Urfé's *L'Astré,* Mlle. de Scudéry's *Le Grand Cyrus,* La Calprenèd's *Cléopâtre,* which continued the *courtois* current of the Middle Ages and gave him, he tells us, "bizarre and romanesque notions of which experience and reflection were never quite able to cure me," though he adds that the *Lives* of Plutarch did "cure me a little of the effects of the novels."

The novels themselves were a strange mixture, because the early seventeenth century had seen a renaissance of Stoicism, and although their heroines were heirs of those of medieval courtly literature, they were in stoic control of themselves. In Tacitus, he found a moralist opposing to the growing profligacy of his time the supposedly virtuous lives of the primitive German tribes. There was also Montaigne, whom he knew well and who in several of his essays had praised primitive peoples. On the other hand there was his deeper Calvinism with its conviction of the total depravity of man.

Like most authors of "great books," Rousseau is thus a reservoir into which flow contradictory currents—in his case the result of the already far-advanced dislocation of Western thought. Besides, in his day, the neopagan mythological exaltation of free love, with Jupiter and Venus as ideals, which developed at the court of Louis XIV, had, in spite of Bossuet, evolved further. It often sank into a low eroticism, or at least into the exaltation of the rationalized hedonism of Horace, whom Voltaire praised for having taught him "to scorn death while enjoying life to the full" (*savourer la vie*). Indeed, he wrote in *Le Mondain:* "I love luxury, and even softness, all pleasures and arts, elegance, taste and ornaments. Every gentleman must have such sentiments."

Rousseau was to formulate the antithesis of that ideal. Voltaire represented the culmination of the epicurean hedonistic side of the pagan renaissance. Mixed with the *courtois* current, it had corrupted even some papal courts and scandalized the plebeian Luther. In spite of the "Catholic reaction" and the renaissance of Stoicism, it had triumphed under Louis XIV and now dominated the arts and manners of aristocratic and high bourgeois circles, to the scandal of the plebeian Rousseau. Rousseau had his own coarser inclinations to vice, as is evidenced in his *Confessions,* but he did have an inoculation of Stoic doctrine, a Calvinistic subconsciousness and a middle-class jealousy.

All this, the announcement of the first Dijon Academy contest deeply stirred. At that date, 1750, he had been in Paris some nine years. Married to a vulgar woman, he was copying music for a living and was in turn attracted and repelled by the life around him. The challenging question: "Did the Arts and Sciences

Contribute to Purify Morals?" reawoke in a flash his Stoic-Calvinistic thought. "They did not," he would say against Voltaire. To hedonism, he would oppose virtue. *La vertu! La vertu!* became his theme, proposed in a style itself a potent mixture of the sentimental tirades of the romantic novels and of the classical love of antithetical periods.

"Virtue I defend," he proclaims at the very beginning. He reveals at once his abysmal ignorance of the Middle Ages, but no sooner has he hailed the Renaissance than he turns against it. His whole future work is latent in this essay. He shows that he already has the idea of some advantages in the lives of primitive peoples: "The American savages who go naked and live through hunting were never put under yoke, for what yoke could be put on men who need nothing?" This thought he will develop in his second essay. Even there, it will not mean, as has so often been said (we shall see on what basis), that he believes in the essential goodness of man. But in this first discourse his uppermost thought is clear: human nature is so far from being naturally good that it needs to be curbed through discipline and renunciation: "Before art had fashioned our manners and taught our passions to speak a studied language, our ways were rustic but natural. . . . Human nature at bottom was no better." And again: "Men are perverse, they would still be worse if they had had the unhappiness of being born learned."

With etiquette came hypocrisy. With the progress of the arts and sciences, virtue fled. He praises the first Persians, the Scythians, the Germans of Tacitus, the Indians of Montaigne, "who were preserved from the contagion of vain knowledge." Particularly does he laud the Spartans: "O Sparta, while vices led by the fine arts entered Athens, you drove them from your walls." So too, the early Romans: "What has become of their thatched roofs and rustic homes where once dwelt moderation and virtue?" All this is, of course, history idealized in favor of his theme, but it is evident that his theme is faith not in the natural goodness of man but in the need of renunciation of luxury. So, when he begins to sketch the growth of the sciences and the arts he pictures it as due to our vices and ending in the debilitating effects of luxury: "Luxury is a sure sign of wealth, but what becomes of virtue when wealth must be sought at all costs?" The outcome will be effeminacy, which opens the door to conquest by the more primitive.

Toward the end comes his condemnation of classical education based on authors who "give children models of bad actions drawn from mythology"; and this leads him to express a thought which will also mature in his next discourse: "Such an education leads to that pernicious inequality introduced among men by the distinctions of talents and the disparagement of virtue." Before closing, he condemns the philosophers of his day. This took courage and is a proof of his sincerity: "One pretends that there are no bodies, another that there is only matter, the only god in the world; another still that men are wolves and may freely devour one another." He condemns by name Hobbes and Spinoza. On the other hand he praises Bacon, Descartes and Newton and picks up the Platonic idea that such men should be the counselors of kings, which may seem contradictory but is an indication of his incipient appreciation of the scientific method and a foreshadowing of the realistic education which he will advocate in his *Émile*.

To condemn the arts and sciences was evidently a hard position to maintain. Refutations came aplenty. Rousseau wavered in his answer to them in at least three essays and in his attempt to live up to his praises of virtue. It would seem that until 1750 Rousseau had been only a casual thinker played on by the many currents mentioned. But his success obliged him to work out a doctrine. At the challenge of the first Dijon contest, his subconscious had flashed out its incoherent content.

But when the Dijon Academy set up its new question: "What Is the Origin of Inequality Among Men?" it was as a prominent champion of ideas that Rousseau felt called on to write. This time he would start consciously to push on the elaboration of a doctrine. The first discourse had been a short and brilliant improvisation, the second was to be a labored construction more than twice as long. This was in the fall of 1753. The article *Political Economy,* which we are also asked to consider, was published in the fall of 1755 in the fifth volume of the *Encyclopédie.* This shows that Rousseau had been led to take up the problem of the role of the state in safeguarding morals. He had just come back from a trip to Geneva; in fact he dedicates his new discourse to its magistrates, showing that their system of government was for him an added incentive to study political questions.

It is not clear why the committee on the Great Books picked up this political economy article for special study, for, as Schinz brings out, it is wholly tentative, and Rousseau even abstains from mentioning it in his *Confessions*. It does show, however, how immature was Rousseau's thought at the time. In this paper he does not utilize the current idea of the social contract which he will later make so famous, nor does he reason on the basis of the natural goodness of human nature. On the contrary, he holds that political organization goes against nature, as it would curb personal in favor of common interests. The problem is how to secure a just government in spite of natural selfishness. Rousseau then eloquently speaks of law as an expression of a general will, but he remains puzzled as to how it came to be that men accepted sacrifice of their personal wills to the general will, their selfish interests to the common good. Nor does he find an answer.

Whereupon he shifts to the question as to the means the sovereign may take to enforce the law. May not the individual elude the magistrate, and may not the magistrate himself disobey the law to his own advantage? The question will continue to haunt Rousseau, and his solution will appear only some nine years later in *The Social Contract*. The article *Political Economy* is then to be considered only as an early and, to him, unsatisfactory phase of his political thought.

We may now turn to the really important second Dijon discourse: *On the Origin of Inequality,* which he was writing about the same time and which is to be the main subject of our study. Is it based on anthropological research? By no means, as in any case the data was unavailable. Rousseau tells us he will use his imagination: "Let us begin," he writes, "by disregarding all the facts," for he recognizes, or at least pretends to, that the state of nature never existed, since God did not leave man in that state after He created him. Yet, immediately after, he adds: "O man, here is your history such as I have read it not in books which lie, but in nature which never does."

After a hint that man's body may have evolved from lower forms, he tells us that he will take him as nature made him. Man in the state of nature was physically strong, agile, frightened perhaps at first, but soon conscious that he could best other animals. But what about infirmities natural to old age? A natural life preserves men from gout and rheumatism, lets them die like the animal without knowing it. "Since nature destined us to be healthy, I almost dare assume that the state of reflection is against nature and that the man who meditates is a depraved animal. . . . All the commodities which men devised are so many particular causes of degeneration." Nudity in hot countries, furs of animals in cold—how ideal; clothes, houses—how unnecessary! Living alone, with nothing to do, but close to danger, the natural man slept long but lightly, was keen of sight, hearing and smell, but had a crude palate and sense of touch.

What about his "metaphysical and moral side"? Like the animal, he is an ingenious machine, but he has a special capacity of choice. Precisely, it is this power which will mean for him the first possibility of depravity, for "the will still calls when nature is mute." Man has also the capacity for perfection, and that too will be a source of misfortune, since otherwise he would remain in his original condition of living tranquilly and innocently, "knowing but physical desires, food, a female, and sleep," without imagination or sentimental feelings, incurious, indifferent, conscious only of the present.

Does Rousseau call this solitary man apathetic, happy because thoughtless, being naturally good, as is so often said? Actually, no. He even specifies: "Having no moral relations or known duties, men could be neither good nor bad, and had neither vices nor virtues." However, Rousseau takes his stand against Hobbes, who asserts that natural man was bad. Rousseau accuses Hobbes of having "credited man in the state of nature with a multitude of passions which are the work of society and rendered law necessary."

On the other hand, Rousseau borrows from Mandeville, although the latter, in his *Fable of the Bees,* translated into French in 1740, held that the luxury and vices of individuals turned to the advantage of society. Mandeville credited man with a sentiment of pity. Rousseau accepts this: "It is certain that pity is a natural sentiment . . . anterior to reflection . . . which even animals have." Here, along with the doctrine of an innate moral sense of Shaftesbury and Hutcheson, is one source of the growth of sentimentality in the eighteenth century which was to affect the Romantic school. It substitutes sentiment for reason: "Socrates," Rousseau writes, "may acquire virtue through reason, but human-kind would have long ceased to exist if its conservation had depended only on reason." Natural animal pity is what makes whatever there may be of goodness in natural man: "With passions so little active, and such a salutary check, men, more bent on preserving themselves from harm than on doing harm to others, living apart and solitary, knew neither vanity, nor esteem, nor scorn, had no notion of mine and thine, and no idea of justice; violence from others being something to stand or repulse, without any idea of punishment or revenge." So natural man was neither good nor bad but, like other animals, had a sense of pity.

Still, what about love? In the state of nature, it is but a natural physical impulse to be satisfied indifferently. In the state of society, love is a fictitious sentiment craftily nurtured by women "to make dominant the sex which should obey."

Here suddenly we get a startling indication of what Rousseau really means by his man in the state of nature: "Love, being based on comparisons which the natural man is unable to make, is practically nonexistent for him; for, since he is unable to form abstract ideas of regularity and proportion, he cannot have sentiments of admiration and love."

This is sound psychology: the animal cannot know love, here evidently considered as based at least partly on rational esteem. But what does this mean if not something which does not seem to be generally realized, that Rousseau's man in the state of nature is not *man* at all, but an ante-homo sapiens, an animal still devoid of reason?

It then appears that as a study of what materialistic evolutionists have to explain—how an animal may develop into an intelligent man, and what would be the life of such a being in the prerational stage of development—this first part of Rousseau's essay may not be without merit. What he is especially bent on showing is that other authors credited man in the state of nature with evil characteristics which, according to him, only living in society could develop. What he wants to do is to get back to man in the real state of nature, and this turns out to be in the state of an amoral, because still irrational, animal nature.

Rousseau was then faced with the difficulty of explaining how his prerational animal could become an intelligent man. He has, to a surprising degree, the conception of evolution through incalculable centuries, but he necessarily remains nonplussed—satisfied, however, that he has at least shown that "inequality is scarcely sensible in the state of nature."

We must therefore come to the startling conclusion about the first part of Rousseau's discourse *On the Origin of Inequality* that in it he really asserts it is better to be an irrational animal than a man. Hence his phrase: "A man who thinks is a depraved animal." Rousseau has merely established that a nonrational animal is not bad, since it lives purely on instinct, which of course is true but takes us wholly out of any discussion about man. If Rousseau's state of nature is so evidently antehuman, it is really irrelevant to the thesis that the development of society has corrupted primitive genuine man and introduced inequality.

We should not be surprised, therefore, to find Rousseau starting all over again in the second part of his discourse, this time contrasting rational primitive man with rational civilized man, which is what he should have done in the first place.

He now begins with the *homme naissant:* man being born, showing again how strongly Rousseau has the evolutionary point of view: a being just passing out of the stage of an animal limited to mere sensations. How will he now make him pass into the rational stage? As was to be expected, he begs the question: "The number of men increasing, life became more difficult. Conditions required more industry. Along waterways men invented the fishing line; in the forest, bows and arrows." His animal man now reasons; he makes the comparisons and generalizations necessary to invent. But how did man get this reasoning power? Rousseau attempts an explanation: "The reiterated application of diverse beings to himself must have engendered the perceptions of certain relations. These relations, which we express by words, produced finally in man some sort of reflection. . . ." This is, of course, putting the cart before the horse: a being must have a spiritual power to be able to abstract universals from particulars, and then judge particulars in terms of universals, the process necessary for invention. But Rousseau dodges this psychological problem by immediately withdrawing his words: ". . . some sort of reflection, or rather a mechanical prudence indicating the most necessary precautions to his safety."

It is on the basis of this contradiction, which must plague all materialistic evolutionists, that Rousseau will develop his primitive man: "The new lights which resulted from this development augmented his superiority over other animals and made him more conscious of it." So, Rousseau goes on, man learned to conserve fire, to invent snares, to become master of the animal world and ever more proud of his species. Experience teaching him that the love of well-being is the only end of human action, he began to distinguish occasions when the common interest could assure him of the help of others from occasions where competition should make him beware. Thus men began to unite in free associations according to their needs, obliging no one permanently. Such were the first mutual engagements based on present and sensible interest. Inarticulate cries, some imitative noises were at first the only means of intercourse. But "after a multitude of centuries" progress could become more rapid. Huts replaced caverns, and thereby a sort of property was acquired, distinct family life became possible, the stronger from the first getting the advantage.

So we reach the second stage of development, the stage we might well have expected Rousseau to begin with, the status of primitive man. The question is again: Does Rousseau say that this primitive man is good? Rather he tells us that he too is neither good nor bad, but certainly at his happiest stage of development. Here we may fully catch Rousseau's real fundamental doctrine: "Nothing is so gentle (*doux*) as man in this primitive state, when placed by nature at equal distances from the stupidity of beasts and the fatal lights of civic man, limited equally by instinct and reason to guarantee himself against the evil which threatens him, restrained by natural pity from harming anyone, even after being harmed [presumably unknowingly] by another."

The naturally good and the happiest man is, then, for Rousseau, neither man in the state of nature nor rational man already somewhat civilized through the use of reason, but man at a supposed intermediary stage between animal instinct and the first use of reason for self-aggrandizement, halfway between the indolence of the merely potential human state and the petulant activity of the self-interest which reasoning will awake. This,

Rousseau thinks, is the stage of development of the savages discovered by explorers and missionaries, this the stage at which
nature intended man to stay, since it made it difficult for him
to evolve further, so much so that in many places, Rousseau
claims, he has not evolved further. In fact it must have been
through chance, fatal chance, that men grew out of that state,
as all further steps, though they may have looked like a perfecting
of the individual, really made for the decrepitude of the species.

But the evolution went on, at least in some nations, those that
became civilized. Family life led to the development of sentiment,
conjugal and paternal love. Man's and woman's work became
differentiated: for woman, the keeping of the hut, for man, the
chase; but, life becoming easier, natural vigor diminished. Some
leisure became possible. New commodities could be acquired
but only made men softer and awake to artificial needs, a first
source of all the evils to come. Community life led to a more
complex language, families began to gather in groups destined
to become tribes and nations. Love became jealousy and shed
blood. Community entertainments developed the beginnings of
the arts, the dance and singing. Differences of performance were
noted, ambition to be the best was born—a step toward inequality
and vice. Vanity and scorn, shame and envy followed. Injured
pride led to bloody revenge. So the happiness of the brute-man
disappeared. Here Rousseau exults: he has refuted those who
hold that man was naturally cruel and needed a police power to
govern him; he has shown that man became so only with the
beginnings of civilization.

The final step in that beginning was the institution of property: "The instant a man needed the help of another, equality
disappeared, property was introduced as provisions were necessary, forests yielded to fields watered by the sweat of men, and
soon slavery and misery were seen to grow with the crops."
"When the first man who enclosed a piece of ground dared to
say: this is mine," writes Rousseau at the beginning of the second
part of this discourse, someone should have cried: "Do not believe this imposter, you are lost if you forget that the fruits of
the earth belong to all, and the earth to no one."

The cultivation of land necessarily brought its partition. Labor
added to the land called for ownership. The result? Again, the
stronger and more skillful got to possess more, and definite social

inequality was stabilized. The process was to go on with the progress of other arts and of language. Gradually, inequalities of talents also led to inequalities of wealth, and wealth to its abuse. With faculties, memory and imagination more active, with reason almost fully developed, self-love waxed stronger, and in its wake came display and pretension, with all the vices they bring. Man, once free and independent, became the slave of his needs or desires and of the people he must have to attain them. Some he will cajole, others threaten. Growing ambition increased rivalry, jealousy, hypocrisy, as the institution of property continued to set loose the profit urge. Property holdings increasing, there were the rich, the poor, domination and servitude, subjugation of neighbors, usurpation and brigandage. With all these passions awakened by the social state stifling natural pity, there ensued a permanent state of war. Thus Rousseau believes he has shown, against Hobbes, that this state of war, far from being due to nature, follows inevitably upon the evolution of the natural animal into the rational man.

How will man rise out of this state of permanent war? As a remedy, Rousseau does not yet stress the current idea of the social contract, but, as in his article on political economy, he has most prominently in mind the appearance of the idea of law. The rich must have realized that their hold on property against natural right was precarious. They then conceived the most significant project "which ever entered the human mind": "Let us submit both the powerful and the weak to mutual duties . . . let us institute a supreme power which may by wise laws protect and defend all the members of the association and keep the peace."

One would expect that Rousseau would accept this as progress. On the contrary, he writes: "Before some equivalent of this proposition, all ran toward their shackles. . . . They could see the advantages of a political establishment but lacked the experience to foresee its dangers." And so, he concludes boldly: "Such was, or must have been, the origin of society and of laws which gave new chains to the weak and new powers to the rich, destroyed forever the liberty of the state of nature, imposed forever the law of property and of consequent inequality, made of an adroit usurpation an irrevocable right, and to the profit of a few ambitious men subjected henceforth all humankind to work, servitude and misery."

As to the development of forms of government: first, some agreement as to laws, then, as these are violated, the choice of an elected magistracy to enforce them, given either to one, to a few or to many. But here is the great point: political organization bred more complex social distinctions and inequalities of credit and power. Out of the disorder loosed by the new play of the old passions of self-love and ambitions sprang despotism, which trampled both the laws and the peoples. Thus the evolution is complete. All are again equal because they are nothing. There is now no law but the will of the despot, or rather his passions.

So Rousseau thinks he has imaginatively led us "independently of the sacred dogmas which gave sovereign authority the sanction of divine right, along the forgotten road which man must have traveled from the state of nature to the political." So he sums up his thesis: "Inequality, being almost null in the state of nature, grows with the development of our faculties and the progress of the human spirit, becomes finally stable and legitimate by the establishment of property and law." In the process, "the original man gradually disappears, society becomes an assemblage of artificial men and fictitious passions, the product of the new social relations and without any true foundation in nature. . . . Man in the state of nature sought only repose, liberty, idleness. The social man, always active, strives till death, courts the great, whom he hates. Honor, friendship, virtues and even vices become a game, as men live for the opinion of others." Laws are violated, and tyranny replaces law. And Rousseau ends his discourse: "It is against the law of nature that a handful of people be surfeited with superfluities while the famished multitude lacks the necessities of life."

It should be easy to see how, with such statements, Rousseau's fundamental doctrine came to be generally expressed: man is naturally good but he was spoiled by social institutions. A close analysis of the second Dijon discourse reveals, nevertheless, that this generalization is totally misleading. What it brings out is that Rousseau's man in the state of nature is no man at all, at most a potentially rational being whose reason is yet undeveloped. He is therefore amoral and lives purely on instinct.

What must be stressed in order to grasp what is really Rousseau's thought is that as soon as this animal attains to reason, he is going to use it for comparisons which will make him ambitious, jealous, and criminal, as he develops higher modes of living guaranteed by private property. He will then get the concept of law, but only to find himself confronted with the problem of enforcing it, abortive solutions which will finally lead to accepted despotism and consecrated inequality. At most was there a tolerable state when man stood between the development of reason and the exclusive use of instinct. Rousseau's man, in the first part of his discourse, is neither good nor bad because he is not a man, and in the second, proportionately bad as he becomes rational.

Rousseau's, then, is the most pessimistic of doctrines. His sentimental side will at times rebel against it. He will then stand opposed to the Calvinistic picture of man as naturally bad; he will, in particular, stress pity as a natural sentiment; but, for Rousseau, while prerational man was amoral, rational man is necessarily immoral. Human reason and human will are but means for the development and the satisfaction of self-love. This is the equivalent of the Calvinistic doctrine of the total depravity of human reason due to the Fall. The Calvinist insists on this depravity to show the absolute need of grace for redemption. Rousseau does not speak of grace, since he purposely disregarded Revelation. It remains to be seen what will be his remedy.

He does not see that remedy as he finishes his article on political economy and his second Dijon discourse. We saw what that remedy was when we studied *The Social Contract*. There only may we catch the consequences of Rousseau's conception of the origin of inequality. As was shown, he continued to reason pessimistically. He remained puzzled as to how the citizen—or the magistrate, for that matter—would accept the general will back of the social contract when that general will would be against his selfish interests, in spite of the argument that since each one is a part of the general will, it can never be against any.

Finally, Rousseau gave up and resorted to a religious sanction, but as he had turned from Christianity, it was the sanction of a deistic creed. The formidable consequence was that he put that sanction in the hands of the state and thus made the state totalitarian, in spite of his fulminations against tyranny.

Still, to see an apostle of freedom such as Rousseau claimed to be, passing on to succeeding generations the principles of socialism and totalitarian communism is not so strange, as there are very few alternatives of thought in any domain, and each has its inescapable consequences. Disregard, as Rousseau tells us he did, the revealed facts about the nature of man, and you must conceive some such evolution as Rousseau describes from the irrational animal stage to the rational and from a primitive life to one fashioned more and more by the lust of sensual pleasures and the lust of power, with consequent injustice and social and international wars. It is true that aristocracies and kings often sought mostly their selfish advantages, that tyrannies developed throughout history and that even today, in the world as a whole, Rousseau's last sentence of the second Dijon discourse is still true: "A handful of people [are] surfeited with superfluities while the famished multitude lacks the necessities of life." Man did constantly put his reason at the service of his passions. If it is a fallacy that "to think is to become a depraved animal," it is true that only man can be depraved, and becomes depraved through the wrong use of reason.

Christian thought must and does recognize all this. It does not believe, however, as Calvinism did, that human nature became wholly corrupt. It has not the consequent Rousseauistic conception that reason will only help the development of injustice, though it holds that even in the natural order man would have needed the help of God to lead a rationally moral life. Christianity does not disown the Greek picture of man seeking virtue through the use of reason and bravely facing the blows of fate. It credits reason with having reached so high a point, particularly with an Aristotle, that it may incorporate many of his findings even into ethics. But it does much more: it goes on speaking of the need of grace to heal wounded human nature and of its further indispensable need for the supernatural life which links man with God and God with man and gives a meaning to suffering. Man is not alone facing an inexorable fate. He is called on to work with God, as God is ready to work with him, to achieve justice on earth as it is in heaven. If there has always been so much evil in the world, it is because of man's failure to do so.

Thus, Christian thought, neither overtrusting nor overdisparaging nature and reason, holds that citizens with trained reasons and wills, conscious of the need of the help of God to curb their passions, can achieve a social and international life in peace through justice. Christian citizens can thus remain free, looking to the state as their instrument in secular pursuits but free for the development of an economic order oriented to the common good, and free to worship God according to His Revelation.

Disown that Revelation, choose Rousseau's alternative of a materialistic evolution of man, and you will have to accept most of his pictures and his conclusions. What brands our times is that those have been so widely accepted. The issue is now between a rebirth of Christian liberty through the recognition of God's order, and Rousseau's totalitarian state.

LOUIS J. A. MERCIER

SELECTED BIBLIOGRAPHY

BABBITT, Irving, *Rousseau and Romanticism*. Houghton, Mifflin.
MARITAIN, Jacques, *Three Reformers*. Scribner.
ROUSSEAU, Jean-Jacques, *Discources*. Random (Modern Library).
MASSON, P. M., *La Religion de J. J. Rousseau*. Paris: Hachette.
SEILLIÈRE, E., *J. J. Rousseau*. Paris: Garnier.
Annales de la Société J. J. Rousseau. Paris: Champion.
The Great Books: A Christian Appraisal, Vol. I. Devin-Adair.
ROUSSEAU, Jean-Jacques, *The Social Contract and Other Essays*. Dutton (Everyman's Library).
ROUSSEAU, Jean-Jacques, *Discourse on Inequality; Treatise on Political Economy*. Regnery.

Kant: Fundamental Principles of the
Metaphysics of Morals

IN SPITE of the twentieth century's coolness toward Kant, it is with a melancholy nostalgia that one reads again his ethical thories. Of course, one no longer reads them with that profound docility that marked an epoch when Kant's nod shook the academic Olympus, for today the father of Transcendentalism has been transcended. But it is still thrilling to discover in our modern edition Kant's fervent enthusiasm for a high and severe morality and catch once more something of his profound appreciation and adoring awe for ethics in its abstract purity. He believed in an eternal morality, the same for all men in all times. He believed that morality was man's first concern and that he had the necessary liberty to make it real in life. These are healthy beliefs, not sufficiently shared in our age.

Why has Kant's work failed to produce a more lasting impression in favor of the sturdy moralism he so loved? The reasons, I think, are three.

First of all, his epistemological commitments hampered him so painfully in his ethical constructions. He knew what he wanted: an ascetical ethic of a high stoic order. Yet he could not appeal to any law outside of himself to impose it, because he had locked his soul out of an intelligible external world. He refused to derive a necessitating force from experience, because he held that experience had none. Yet he disdained a shifting morality to be constructed on the empirical basis of trial and error, and so he had to derive a universally valid ethic from his imprisoned solitary soul.

This herculean task required a subtle and sinuous analytical

tactic of explaining man's moral consciousness in terms so original and personal that few men recognize the Kantian conscience
as anything like their own. The wearisome obscurity of the
Kantian dialectical process so confuses the simple student and
so irritates the trained moral philosopher that the final result
for both is impatient vexation. Kant's unshakable conviction that
the human will was free, coupled with his simultaneous reluctance to affirm it without hedging because of his epistemological
position, makes him do a tightrope dance that produces dizziness
in the awed spectator.

Either the will is free or it is not. Between affirmation and
negation there is a chasm so wide that nothing will bridge it,
least of all ambiguous affirmations shot through with principles
that deny them. This was probably the greatest tragedy in Kant's
whole philosophical life. It explains his developed dexterity in
leaping to and from the phenomenological and the noumenal
sides of being—both of which were far more Kantian than real.
It is true that it helped finally to achieve a logically coherent
system in which he could postulate human freedom without admitting it, but this coherence was characterized by such a swaying
equilibrium it did not suggest that rugged stability which is
necessary for an effective morality.

In like manner his voluntary exile from objective reality made
him build up a strange notion of moral necessity. Kant insists
that morality, the famous categorical imperative, is a law. He also
sees clearly that the effect of law is necessity. Yet he cannot admit
that this moral necessity is derived from beyond the self, so he
makes necessity flow from the autonomous will. This makes the
lawmaker and the subject of law identical. The sage of Koenigs-
berg never mentions the principle known in jurisprudence since
the days of Rome, namely, that the lawmaker is not necessitated
by his own law, which is expressed in the English tradition by
the more vivid phrase: the king can do no wrong. Even the man
on the street who is not versed in juridical philosophy knows
that he who makes the law will change it whenever he sees fit, and
he will do so when circumstances make it convenient. Kant's
moral law is self-imposed. It arises from freedom, and as he himself says, it is unthinkable except as a product of freedom. Such
a binding can carry with it no greater necessity than that of a free
resolution.

So it is that the fundamental expression of Kantian morality, *act as if the maxim of thy action were to become by thy will a universal law of nature,* is not really a law at all. It is a counsel of perfection, for it would be lovely if we all did that, but Kant never once showed that this principle was anything more than a consummation devoutly to be wished.

The second reason for the lack of survival value in Kantian ethics is the poverty of its guidance. Beyond the general principle mentioned above—which Kant repeats at least a hundred times— and a few cases which he solves by the hazy application of his principle, we have no more detailed norm of action. The practical value of the Kantian law in the concrete will be equal to a man's vision of what he wants nature to be. I wonder if any two men have the same vision of that blessed state, or whether one and the same man has the same vision through successive periods of his life. Even at any given moment, when our vision is for an instant stable and definite, it is hardly so detailed that it will include all the possible actions of man. Whatever can be said in favor of the Kantian guiding principle, it certainly is evident that it cannot give rise to a moral system. It is a glorious norm that can have no practical meaning. On last analysis, the Kantian principle meant that a conduct is moral if it came up to Kant's desire. This would be a lofty comportment, indeed, but it is hard to see why I should live as Kant desires, and it is still harder to know what Kant might want in any given contingency.

The third factor that weakens Kant's influence is the more or less patent conflict between the implicit dynamism of his work and the explicit methodic that he imposed on it. He is straining to derive a morality uniform for all men, and to do so he must derive it from the one thing common to all, their nature. He cannot fall back on nature as we find it in experience, because this is always vitiated by the limitations of the empirical subject. He therefore does again what Plato, Aristotle and Aquinas had done before him. He and they use ideal nature and declare it to be the ultimate norm of morality.

For Kant's illustrious predecessors nature was an objective

reality grasped ontally by the mind. It has a structure which necessitated irrational things blindly and human minds rationally, leaving men the possibility of acting irrationally in their contributions to the sum total of natural activity. Such a notion of nature could be detailed because it was not the product of wishful thinking but the object of serene contemplation. A complete system of ethics could be erected and Kant really accepted it. His strange attitude toward reality, which he had divided against itself by phenomenal and noumenal tensions, simply did not give Kant the right to subscribe to classical morality, though he thought he must and was anxious to do so. In order to legitimize his acceptance, he reerected the ancient thought structure so that every bolt and beam had to be translated to another position in order to give the appearance of being a new edifice.

The effort bespeaks genius but leaves the student nonplussed. Either Kant was saying the same as the older philosophers, and if so, why deny it and why go through such arduous huffing and puffing only to produce what had already existed; or he was saying something different, and if so, where lay the difference and how had his gothic structure improved on its classical counterpart? This dilemma is more palpable today than ever, and the years have not found a solution but rather have confirmed earlier suspicions that there was none. The Kantian moral problem will never be solved by the Kantian epistemological method. Therein lies the disservice which Kant did to the thing he loved best, ethics. His epistemology is implicit in modern thought, and by it he has destroyed in our time any hope of achieving a universally acceptable moral code. There is a sad irony in this, because Kant formulated his noetic in order to make it an eternal defense of ethics.

Kant's passing from the center of the philosophical stage is due to his incapacity to hold his audience. In his case, as in many others, the instrument he forged for a determined task has been found inadequate, but its utility in other fields is supposed. The morality which he preached and was for him his great mission has been abandoned, and the deadly sharp tool he made to carve it is used today for ends he would have abhorred. If only our generation would see that if the tool could not shape the thing for which it was made, it could hardly be applied with wholesome effect to objects not one whit less important than conduct!

The foregoing reflections were made in terms of an immanent critique. Such procedure is the only just method for evaluating any work of thought. However, it is not the only critique possible, and in a theory of conduct it is not the only critique desirable. Any vision of morality by its very pretensions must have direct influence on man's external action, which is the life of the community. For society Kantian moral philosophy is a dangerous thing. It is dangerous because it is an ineffective stimulus toward desirable conduct, and it is more dangerous yet because it does not give the community a voice in the determination of ethical goodness in the concrete. In other words, Kant is more of an obstacle than a help in the maintenance or reformation of communal comportment. If Kantian ethics were the only moral philosophy at the disposal of society, it would logically mean the end of human living together. These accusations are made from the pragmatical viewpoint, but it is wise to bring them to the attention of students of morality, so that they see what a commitment to Kantian ethicism brings with it on the practical level.

The first practical accusation we made was that Kantian doctrine is no effective moral stimulus for the majority of the community. For Kant, the true aim of life was moral activity. Morality was never a means to anything. It was man's end in this life and it was his true mission, so that all else was indifferent and secondary. The ethical imperative could not be questioned, nor may man dispute with it. It made itself known by a spontaneous inner command that needed no justification in terms of reason or of practical consequences. What conscience dictates must be fulfilled and only because conscience dictates it. This is the essence of Kantian morality.

Now, it is the experience of any man, and acutely of those who have studied humanity, that the individual accepts moral urges with something less than enthusiasm. Even the best of us make shady compromises with duty sincerely accepted. The Freudians, in their mythological explanation of conscience, propose duty as a self-inflicted repression of natural desire arising from the Oedipus complex. It is hardly my intention to defend this explanation, but I willingly admit that it is a more adequate expression of man's attitude to conscience than Kant's Olympian pure ego that speaks with regal calm to an adoring moral subject. Although we like morality in general, we dislike its particular application to our lives in the concrete here and now. If the true motive for obeying the concrete commands of conscience is the desirability of obeying them for themselves, then the vast majority of men will cease to obey. We do not, speaking in general, find the performance of duty desirable for itself, and yet, according to Kant, we must do our duty precisely because that is man's supreme good.

Kant was not speaking to the ordinary mortal. He himself may have been one of humanity's rare specimens who are moved to correct action because correct action appeals to them above all else. However, the average good man of the community has to be enticed to moral effort by some other motive. The existence of police forces and the fear of our fellows' censure prove conclusively that men need much more than the voice of conscience to make them good. The community, because it simply must have a minimum of morality in order to live, is not very squeamish about the motives that induce men to right action. It hands out reward for virtue and penalty for vice, because it knows that without such pressure the morality needed for communal existence will not be forthcoming. In its practical existence, society professes no faith in the Kantian theory of ethics.

Not only is this the position of society. Each individual knows that the moral imperative is a stumbling block to his peace of mind. One of the most stirring passages in the world's literature is St. Paul's description of his despairing battle with the Law which finally defeated him (Rom. 7, 12-25). His great relief came when he found the message of Christianity, whereby he could be saved from the Law because he would be elevated above it by Christ, to whom he bound himself by effective and dynamic love. There are few individuals who will not recognize in St. Paul's picture their own experience. We strive to be moral; we labor and we groan; yet we fail. Too intense a preoccupation with moral perfection has put many a man into a sanatorium. The desire to be moral, no matter how fervent, has never yet made a moral man, and I would not hesitate to include Kant in this generalization.

There is needed a higher motivation, and whatever it may be, it will always entail a love of something more tangible and more palpable than pure morality; love of God, love of the neighbor, love of the fatherland. In all these three cases there is an object above morality which has our spontaneous allegiance and which can effectively make us moral. Yet, according to Kant, such action is immoral because it is done for a motive other than a desire to be moral for its own sake. Kant never understood the role of love in human life nor could he understand that it was the driving force in the universe. He knew so much, but he did not know that it is love that makes the world go 'round, and not a categorical imperative.

The second accusation was that the community, in Kant's system, would have no part in determining what is moral and what is not. This is a graver accusation than the first, as far as practical consequences are concerned. Morality, for Kant, was utterly subjective. It was the autonomous ego dictating to the individual citizen and excluding any other determining voice. The isolation of this authority is not lessened by the counsel that we must so act that the maxim for our action can be proposed as a universal norm. It is still left to the individual to decide what should be a universal law. He, and he alone, must decide, and he will decide in terms of his own spontaneous decrees of conscience. If there should be a clash between his decree and that of the community, the communal decree must be ignored. The community has no court to which it can appeal against the individual, for there can be no other court of appeal than the imperative of his own ego.

Such doctrine makes the very concept of society moral or immoral. Society, in order to exist, must make demands on its members. These demands must bind in conscience. If occasionally there arises a clash between personal and social ethics, there must be some arbiter, neither the individual nor society, to which both can go for judgment. There must be some objective norm for conduct, and society must have the power to command.

In the Kantian position, society cannot command with the voice of authority. It can only woo the approval of the spontaneous and uncaused dictamen of its subject. If this dictamen be favorable, then society can oblige, not because of any authority it possesses but by reason of the untouchable authority of the individual. If society urges an authority of its own over the citizen's activity, Kant declares it immoral. If this is so, society ceases to be an entity in its own right, and in the best of conditions it will be the mere resultant of the casual accord of the categorical imperatives of the individuals who live in the same territory. In the worst of conditions, since society in order to function will coerce its members without waiting for the autonomous decree of the individual's conscience, the community is acting outside the field of ethics. The concepts of civic law and social morality simply become nonsensical in this scheme. Jurisprudence ceases to be subject to morality, because it deals with laws not derived exclusively from the solitary ego. Is it not from this Kantian concept of morality that we have the modern positivistic theory of law, which divorces legislation from ethics and relates it exclusively to the state's capacity for coercion?

It is not mere whimsy to see in this doctrine a rationalization of Luther's belief that the powers of this world were evil, tolerated by God to punish the wicked and try the good. Subjectivism in all its forms: religious, philosophic and esthetical, must inevitably ignore the social aspect of man, and such a process weakens the community, which is no less a reality that the individual himself. Kant did not want such a conclusion, but the dynamism of logic was stronger than Kant's good will.

The unsocial coloring of Kantian ethics has its historical roots. The eighteenth century was a period that rose to the defense of the human person against the absolutism of kings. As in all noble campaigns of mankind, the position of the individual became extreme in order to fight its extreme antithesis. However, it is rarely the role of truth to occupy extreme positions. In our day, thought is occupied in attacking the absolutism of the individual, and, of course, communism is the extreme opponent to our modern despot. Kant was responsible in no small degree for the victory of the autonomous individual over the absolute king, but his victory saddled society with no kinder a tyrant. The Kantian theory is hardly an apt instrument in our time for the eternal struggle of reason against evil. Nor do our contemporaries feel the slightest inclination to use it.

GUSTAVE WEIGEL

SELECTED BIBLIOGRAPHY

MARÉCHAL, J., S.J., *Le Point de départ de la métaphysique. Cahier III, La Critique de Kant.* Bruges, Paris.

WARD, J., *A Study of Kant.* Cambridge.

FOUILLÉE, A., *Le Moralisme de Kant et l'amoralisme contemporaine.* Paris.

MESSER, A., *Kant's Ethik.* Leipzig.

SCOTT, J., *Kant on the Moral Life.* Macmillan.

JONES, W., *Morality and Freedom in the Philosophy of Immanuel Kant.* Oxford.

KANT, IMMANUEL, *Preface to the Metaphysical Elements of Ethics.* Regnery.

Nietzsche: Beyond Good and Evil

SINCE NIETZSCHE was not a systematic philosopher, it is not an easy task to present his thought in a summary, and impossible to construct a neat outline with the label: this is what Nietzsche taught. Reading Nietzsche today with the history of the past ten years fresh in our minds, it is easy enough to dismiss him as the nineteenth-century prophet of Hitlerism. Yet, though there is a strong connection between what Nietzsche thought and said and what Hitler did, it is equally true that Nietzsche would have been just as uncomfortable under Hitler as any good democrat. It is also easy to label him as an immoralist, an atheist, a nihilist. In each of these labels there is an element of truth, but none of them would provide a valid clue to the man or his thought. It is only when they are taken in terms of his set purpose and in terms of his own life that they can be applied.

More, probably, than any other philosopher, Nietzsche elevated personal experience into a philosophy, universalized it, preached it. Every philosopher, of course, attempts to interpret experience, beginning with the facts of sensible and intellectual experience and reaching a final understanding of these facts by means of principles implicit in the recognition of them. This process, however, though it is a highly personal effort, is not egotistic, since experience is interpreted not according to the personal whims of the philosopher but according to its objective meaning.

Nietzsche did not bother himself with this preoccupation of philosophers but took his own denials, moods and inner conflicts as his starting point, looked at them against the background of the moral, political and religious mediocrity of the nineteenth century, and announced not so much a new philosophy as a new man who must emerge if culture is to survive. There is, consequently, more of Nietzsche in his philosophy than there is, for instance, of Aristotle in Aristotelianism or of Kant in Kantianism; and correspondingly greater difficulty in understanding Nietzsche. The purpose of this article is merely to provide a key to the understanding of *Beyond Good and Evil.*

This work is a companion piece of the more famous *Thus Spake Zarathustra,* and repeats in less poetical and less ecstatic language the main themes of Zarathustra. Together, these two works represent the most mature and the most deliberate of all Nietzsche's writings. *Beyond Good and Evil* was originally intended to be the first part of Nietzsche's masterpiece, *The Will to Power: Attempt at the Transvaluation of All Values.* Both will to power and transvaluation of values are at the root of Nietzsche's thought; both ideas appear again and again in the pages of *Beyond Good and Evil.* An understanding of these essential notions will serve as a key to the work as a whole.

The will to power, as Nietzsche understood it, is not identified with brute force, power politics, mere ruthlessness, though it does connote all of these. The nearest synonym of this will is independence, though this term also takes on a peculiarly Nietzschean sense. Will is identified with life, and life in the full sense means independence from accepted norms of conduct. To live and to exercise the will to power is to be freed from the restraints of moral, religious, political institutions. This is not an apology for license or immorality in the accepted sense, but a state of natural perfection to be achieved by the ideal man, the superman, who by sheer force of will raises himself above the tensions of everyday existence. In this completely naturalistic ideal state of man, the superman will differ from the ordinary man just as the ordinary man differs from the ape. The concept is rooted in a denial of God, of the supernatural, of Christianity and based upon an insight into the secret forces behind human activity, which, Nietzsche tells us, is the most profound insight that ever revealed itself to daring travelers and adventurers (Cf. *Beyond Good and Evil,* n. 23, Modern Library Edition, p. 26).

Life, as Nietzsche lived it, was a series of heartbreaking disappointments and of mounting tensions. He was the son of a Lutheran pastor, and his early years were spent in an atmosphere of piety. His first ambition as a scholar was to become a theologian, according to the tradition of his family, but early contact with the higher criticism destroyed his faith, and the reading of Schopenhauer confirmed him in atheism. He turned then to his second scholarly love, philology, acquired an enduring admiration of Greek culture and, after brilliant early successes, became a professor of philology at the age of twenty-four.

His career was interrupted first by military service and then permanently by ill health. During these early years he formed deep friendships, most of them later turning to bitter enmity. The most famous of these was his friendship with Wagner. In defense of Nietzsche's erstwhile friends, it might be mentioned that most of them did not themselves understand the reasons for the rifts and were as puzzled by Nietzsche's attitudes toward themselves as Nietzsche himself was puzzled by what he considered their failure toward himself. The fact is that he was never friendless in the superficial sense, as was evident when madness overtook him, since there were always many ready to stand by and assist him. He was, he felt, friendless in the deeper sense that he had no one with whom he could share his deepest feelings and his innermost thoughts; it never occurred to him that it might possibly be the very nature of those feelings and thoughts that repelled.

Moreover, he did not take friends as they were, but measured them by absolute standards and found them wanting. He expected his friends to become his disciples, to subordinate themselves and their interests to his self-imposed mission, and it was precisely this mission that none of them could accept. This failure to find friends was of great importance during the years of his major productivity: it accentuated his feeling of isolation and increased in proportion his conviction of being a man with a great and unique mission in the world; it contributed to that feeling of egotistical superiority so noticeable in his writings. The chapter headings of his last work, *Ecce Homo*, reveal more eloquently than any explanation his egotism: *Why I Am So Wise; Why I Am So Clever; Why I Write Such Excellent Books.*

From the heights of this morbid egotism Nietzsche looked out upon the world and saw that it was not good. German culture in particular and European culture in general were to him an abomination. It included education, literary appreciation, artistic standards, art, music and left out the essential element, life. This element, self-possession, which means striving, the strenuous will, should dominate knowledge; the fact was that knowledge was dominating it. It was a subservient culture with no real values, as was evident to Nietzsche, and to us as well, in the glorification of the German military victory in the Franco-Prussian war and in the consequent identification of culture with success. Germans, he thought, knew about culture but they did not live it; their knowledge was an historical ruin. This vision of complacent mediocrity stirred the indignation of Nietzsche, and he set himself the purpose of destroying it and with it all the human institutions that had contributed to its existence: religion, morality, democracy—all of them, in his view, instruments of mediocrity.

This, briefly, was life as Nietzsche lived it. Life, as he saw it, was something far more perfect. It is not to be confined within the limits set by democratic morality, bourgeois customs or humanitarian religion. Life is Willing. Willing is neither simple nor evident, but a highly complicated combination of sensations, thoughts, emotions, which present an apparent but deceptive unity in the act of willing. Will is the true driving force, and once recognized as such and separated from the popular fallacies surrounding it, once accepted for itself and fostered, it can raise man to the stature of the superman. It is the only causality, and conscience commands us to explain everything by will: the world is will to power (see n. 19).

Freedom of will is not the petty power to pick and choose, to do this or that at the dictates of whim, as religion and morality would have it. It is a complex state of delight on the part of the person exercising volition, or the will to power. The person commands and identifies himself with the executor of the order; he triumphs over obstacles and thinks that it is his own will that overcomes them. In this self-identification and self-realization he resolves all his tensions and achieves that kind of warlike peace that is the prerogative of the superman. Individuals may at one time or another experience this keen delight of will, but only the few, the philosophers, will achieve it as a constant state (see n. 36).

This is the center of Nietzsche's thought, his insight into the absolute. It controls his interpretation of history, his criticism of all human institutions, his attack on Christianity and morality. From this point of view it is possible to undertake a criticism of his criticism of accepted human values. Truth and falsity, good and evil, moral and immoral, certain and uncertain, all of these opposites express certain preferences and therefore certain values for the ordinary man. They are in fact necessary for him; and the ordinary man, the herd, is necessary as well. He must and will exist always, but only as a necessary condition for the superman. Herd values are not ultimate nor final. Beyond all of them there is an area to be touched only by the great, and the dimensions of this greatness are those of will and willing. In this stratospheric retreat true freedom will be discovered, as opposed to the specious freedom of the herd: it is the emotion of supremacy resulting from commanding. "True freedom will not be found in the stupid democratic sense, but beyond good and evil: in solitude" (see n. 23).

Nietzsche took all the institutional forms of human organization as manmade, including Christianity. He accused them all of being somewhat deliberate attempts on the part of the strong to exercise in a minor and mistaken way the will to power. The leaders, therefore, were the more guilty, for they, more than the led, might have realized the will to power in its purity. The entire system, and especially religion and more particularly Christianity, must be destroyed or at least superseded—by the ideal man of Nietzsche.

By a curious logical inversion Nietzsche, having begun with the idea of the superman and the will to power, distinguishes three periods of history: the premoral period, during which action was valued from consequences; the moral period, during which action is valued by intention; the ultramoral period, during which action will be valued by something surmounting moral intention (see n. 32). The fact that the last is an ideal state to be achieved does not worry Nietzsche. But perhaps it is unfair to criticize Nietzsche from the point of view of logical correctness, since logic, and the truth which it serves, are values of the herd with which he cannot be bothered.

A more appropriate criterion, perhaps, granting Nietzsche's point of departure, is that of viewing his thought in relation to the contemporary scene. From this point of view it is possible to credit him with certain valid contributions. It is certainly to his credit that he was sensitive to the shallowness of contemporary culture and courageous enough to speak out against it. The late nineteenth century was a period of crude materialism and easy optimism. Religion, in the forms in which Nietzsche knew it, had been degraded to humanitarianism and identified its purposes with those of the state or of material success. Art in its various forms spent itself in glorifying the transient values of commercial or military success and thereby really divorced itself from life. Himself more of an artist than a thinker, Nietzsche had reason to be impatient with what he saw about him.

It is also to his credit that he recognized suffering as a vital and necessary factor of life and that he preached it to a superficial age. This is probably one of the deepest motives of Nietzsche, though he himself might not have been fully aware of its importance in his own work. His break with Wagner was due to the realization that in *Parsifal* Wagner had adopted a Christian explanation of suffering. While this brought forth some of his most blasphemous tirades, it cannot be denied that fundamentally Nietzsche was occupying himself with a great human problem.

Finally, and still on the credit side, implicit in his program for the superman and the will to power is a demand for a forgotten virtue: greater spiritual discipline and less dissipation of true talent and true values; a demand for greater naturalness in a good sense and less artificiality.

The moral philosopher is usually concerned with analysis, not precisely with making men better. Nietzsche was primarily concerned with the promotion of a new type of man. His moral philosophy is not scientific, analytic and static, but is assertive, exhortatory, dynamic. Had he been able to discipline himself and had he not taken himself and his half-formed ideas as the measure of the real, he might well have been one of the very great philosophers of all time. This impression is confirmed by the frequent experience of finding startling instances of psychological penetration in his writings. It is this power of unmasking hidden motives of action that more than any other quality of his writing makes one feel that perhaps Nietzsche has something to say.

Unfortunately, together with a mind capable of the highest scholarly attainments, Nietzsche possessed a temperament utterly inconsistent with the pursuit of scholarship. He remains a living philosopher not for any great synthesis that he effected, nor for any great doctrines that he proclaimed, but for the intensity and power with which he expressed himself against the superficiality of his own age. As long as that superficiality remains, and we have not seen its end, Nietzsche will wield his influence. Neither in his own day nor in ours is his solution accepted; but then and now his accurate feeling for the emptiness of that which poses as culture awakens a response in thoughtful readers.

CHARLES DENECKE

SELECTED BIBLIOGRAPHY

REYBURN, H. A., *Nietzsche, the Story of a Human Philosopher*. Macmillan.

COPLESTON, Frederick, S.J., *Friedrich Nietzsche, Philosopher of Culture*. London: Burns, Oates & Washbourne.

WEBER, Alfred, *Farewell to European History* (translated by R. F. C. Hill). Yale University.

Nietzsche, Friedrich, The Philosophy of. Random (Modern Library).

NIETZSCHE, Friedrich, *Beyond Good and Evil*. Regnery.

Mill: Representative Government

To UNDERSTAND a man's philosophy we must first understand his background. For there is more to it than appears in his books. A philosopher, like any other mortal, is very much a man of his times. Try as he may, he cannot stand above the stream of history, untouched and unmoved by the currents of thought and the pressure of social movements which take place around him. It is these currents, this pressure, that often determine the growth and direction of one's philosophy. In John Stuart Mill's case, they also explain his blind spots and inconsistencies.

He was born in London in 1806 just as the Industrial Revolution was gathering momentum, and democratic ideas were on the march. He was the eldest son of James Mill. To his father he was more than a son. He was his father's spiritual offspring, his intellectual creation. And to the end of his days John S. Mill remained, to a great extent, a mental reproduction of James Mill, who in turn was the mental reproduction of Jeremy Bentham. In 1812, when John was only six, the elder Mill wrote to Bentham: "Should I die, one thought that would pinch me most sorely would be leaving the poor boy's mind unmade. . . . I take your offer seriously [an offer apparently to be the boy's mental nurse and guardian], and then we may perhaps leave him a successor worthy of both of us." This was the tragedy of John S. Mill—from childhood he was brought up to be a Benthamite reformer, an apostle of utilitarianism.

He had no other teacher but his father; he went to no other school but what he might call today the School of Great Books. At the age of three he was taught Greek by his father, and by the time he was eight he had already read Xenophon's *Anabasis* and *Cyropaedia;* the *Memorials* of Socrates, the whole of Herodotus, the first six dialogs of Plato. In history he had read Plutarch, Robertson, Hume, Gibbon, Watson, Burnet, Hooke,

Millar and Mosheim. At eight he added Latin to Greek, and by the time he was fourteen he had read the works of Virgil, Horace, Phaedrus, Livy, Sallust, Terence, Cicero, Homer, Thucydides, Demosthenes, Aeschines, Lysias, Theocritus, Anacreon, Aristotle, Tacitus, Juvenal, Quintilian and Plato.

His own estimate of the kind of education he received is illuminating. "If I have accomplished anything [he says in his *Autobiography*], I owe it to the fact that through the early training bestowed on me by my father, I started, I may fairly say, with an advantage of a quarter of a century over my contemporaries." He was not blind, however, to his deficiencies. "The deficiencies [he goes on] in my education were principally in the things which boys learn from being turned out to shift for themselves, and from being brought together in large numbers. . . . As I had no boy companions, my amusements were mostly solitary . . . of a quiet if not a bookish turn. . . . I consequently remained inexpert in anything requiring manual dexterity; my mind as well as my hands did its work lamely when it was applied to the practical details. . . . The education which my father gave me was in itself much more fitted for training me to *know* than to *do*."

This, of course, helps to explain a lot of things. For instance, Mill's overoptimistic belief in the power of education as a panacea for all our social ills. He was steeped in Plato, if we remember; and Plato's supreme belief was that virtue is knowledge. Again, being of an impractical cast of mind, but an ardent political reformer withal, he was enthusiastic in his advocacy for the untried method of proportional representation and what we might call "educationally" weighted votes. This, he claimed, was the only way of preserving the real blessings of democracy. He was a sincere, honest, fair-minded man. Where then did he get his strong bias against religion and all priestly caste? He himself tells us where. He says in his *Autobiography:* "I was brought up from the first without any religious belief. . . . It would have been inconsistent with my father's ideas and feelings respecting religion: and he impressed upon me from the first, that the manner in which the world came into existence was a subject on which nothing was known: that the question, 'Who made me?' cannot be answered. . . . I am thus one of the very few examples, in this country, of one who has, not thrown off religious belief, but never had it."

As for his utilitarian philosophy, we know where he derived it—from Bentham and from his own father. And yet, being of a nobler and more refined nature, of a more cultured and receptive mind than either Bentham or his father, J. S. Mill came in time to cherish ideals unknown to both; and in his maturer years he was not quite ready to push the principles of utilitarianism to their ultimate conclusions. For instance, in Bentham's philosophy the principle of majority ("The greatest happiness, *i.e.*, pleasure, for the greatest number") was a simple matter of counting heads.

J. S. Mill revolted from this crude principle. He had picked up somewhere along the line, probably from his acquaintance with Coleridge and the Coleridgians of his time, "sentimental" concepts of duty and rights and order based not so much on the essential nature of things as on the hierarchy of pleasures in man. There are pleasures and pleasures, he said. We must assign to the pleasures of the intellect, of the feelings and imagination and of the moral sentiments, a much higher value as pleasures than to those of mere sensation. It is quite compatible with the principle of utility to recognize the fact that some kinds of pleasure are more desirable and more valuable than others. A being of higher faculties requires more to make him happy, even as he is capable of more acute suffering, than beings of a lower grade of existence.

He did not quite see it, but the fact is that in admitting a natural hierarchy of pleasure, he was parting with Bentham and the Benthamism of his youth. He was admitting that man could be happier in one way with less pleasure than he would be in another way with more. In other words, that happiness is not one with pleasure nor can it be morally calculated in terms of pleasure. Here we need not go out of our way to prove the absurdity of utilitarianism, whether of the crude type like Bentham's, or of the refined type like Mill's. It is enough to note that Mill in later years was inconsistent with the utilitarian principles of his youth. This inconsistency was due in part to his intense loyalty to the memory of Bentham and of his father, even while he found it impossible to square their principles with the facts and problems he had to face. He was trying to patch new cloth unto an old garment and pour new wine into old bottles. It could not be done.

It could not be done, because James Mill was a born pessimist; and J. S. Mill was by nature an optimist—a dreamer who sincerely believed that "all the sources of human suffering are in a great degree conquerable by human effort, though their removal be grievously slow, and a long succession of generations will perish in the breach. . . ." James Mill was a convinced atheist, who could not believe in God, because there were evils in the world; J. S. Mill, on the other hand, had no convictions on the matter, and every tragic experience of his life—the death of his wife and that of his friend Sterling—was driving him closer and closer toward belief in God. In 1860 he was actually groping toward some form of theism when he wrote: "It would be a great improvement to most persons . . . if they firmly believed the world to be under the government of a Being, who willing only good, leaves evil in the world solely in order to stimulate human faculties by an unremitting struggle against every form of it." Unconsciously, he was struggling to shake off the shackles of attitudes and prejudices imposed on him by his father. In this he did not succeed completely, nor did he completely fail. He compromised, and the price of it was inconsistency. But when one starts with false premises, inconsistency is a blessing. It was a blessing, therefore, that J. S. Mill, whose basic philosophy was Bentham's utilitarianism, was inconsistent with it in many ways when he wrote in 1861 his *Considerations on Representative Government*.

Here we are concerned only with the first six chapters. (The book has eighteen chapters: the first six constitute what we might call Mill's political philosophy; the remaining twelve constitute his political science—the political institutions which, in his opinion, would best carry out in English setting the principles of his political philosophy.) He first poses the question: is government a matter of choice? There were in his day two current views on the matter. The first was the so-called "natural law" theory of Locke and Rousseau—government is purely a matter of convention, of social contract. Men could set it up and pull it down at will; they could, therefore, design it in any fashion they pleased. The other view was that of the historical school, expressed thus by its great champion Karl von Savigny: "The motley world of legal forms, like language, art, mores, does not evolve in virtue of deliberate natural reflection or reasoned considerations of utility; it springs rather from the common conviction of the people, from the feeling of inner necessity which excludes all thought of fortuitous and arbitrary origin."

To Mill's credit, he avoids either extreme. He denies the fatalistic view of the historical school, which claimed that the form of government is not at all subject to choice but is predetermined by a people's history and character. On the other hand, he also parts with Locke and Rousseau when he admits certain conditions which limit the people's choice, namely: "The people for whom the government is intended must be willing to accept it; they must be willing and able to do what is necessary to keep it standing; they must be willing and able to do what it requires of them to enable it to fulfill its purposes." In other words, he admits that not every form of government is suitable to every people. What is good for one may be bad for another. Governments, therefore, cannot be put up and pulled down at will according to Bentham's principle of utility or Locke's *Treatise on Government*.

This is perfectly in harmony with sound Christian tradition. The state, though a matter of convention as to its actual existence and the form of government it should adopt, is yet as to its essence a natural institution, a thing willed and defined by the Author of nature. As Burke puts it: "Government is a contrivance of human wisdom to provide for human wants"; but he also says: "He who gave our nature to be perfected by our virtue willed also the necessary means of its perfection. He willed therefore the state." Hence men must agree to form a state, and yet whether this state should have this kind of government or that—whether it be a monarchy, aristocracy or democracy—is for the people to decide in the light of practical wisdom. That is why, to quote Burke again, "the science of government being so practical in itself, and intended for such practical purposes, a matter which requires experience, and even more experience than any person can gain in his whole life, however sagacious and observing he may be, it is with infinite caution that any man ought to venture upon pulling down an edifice which has answered in any tolerable degree for ages the common purpose of society, or of building it up again without models and patterns of approved utility before his eyes."

That Mill was not entirely devoid of these sound principles of experience is quite clear from chapters I and IV, where he admits that there are social conditions under which representative government would be inapplicable. For such an ardent reformer as Mill this was quite an admission to make. In his youth he would never have made it; but when he wrote *Representative Government* he was already a man of fifty-four: he had reached the age of disillusionment; he had seen much since his Benthamite youth and he had learned that democracy, for all its advantages, was not an unmixed blessing.

In chapters II and III, Mill expounds his reasons for his belief that, under the three conditions mentioned above, representative government is ideally the best form of government. There is, of course, nothing original or startling about this doctrine, but Mill's approach to the subject is quite fresh and stimulating, and in these days when one hears so much about the blessings of the welfare state, we might perhaps look profitably into the sound and healthy individualism which he advocates throughout the book.

What is the criterion of a good form of government? This is the question Mill asks himself. Ultimately this question resolves itself into this: what are the ends of government? Is it order? Is it progress? Or is it both? There is no mistaking where Mill's sympathies would lie, were he reduced to a choice of one or the other. He is an apostle of progress. To him, humanity must always be on the march to broader and sunnier heights. On the other hand he seems to have a very narrow and stunted concept of order. In him or in any philosopher who does not possess a true and clear notion of human nature, this is hardly surprising. To him, order is reduced to "obedience" or to "the preservation of peace by the cessation of private violence." It is merely an order imposed *ab extrinseco*. It is not an order demanded *ab intrinseco* by the nature of man in his relation to God, to himself and to his fellow men. It is static order, such as obtains in things mechanical; not dynamic order, such as presides over the rational unfolding of man.

But taking Mill's view as a whole, this is really a minor point. For, after all, he admits that progress presupposes order, permanence. We must hold on to what we have even as we strive for more;

but we must always strive for more, we must always be on the march, for to stand still is to fall behind. In more sober terms Burke expressed the same belief when he said: "A state without the means of some change is without the means of its conservation. Without such means it might even risk the loss of that part of the constitution which it wished most religiously to preserve." What then are the ends of government? Mill sums them all up in the "promotion of the mental advancement of the community, including under that phrase advancement in intellect, in virtue, and in practical activity and efficiency." On the whole this is a sound view. The government is meant to perfect man, that is, to aid him reach, as he would never otherwise reach, the full development of his human nature. This is not saying, of course, that the government's end is directly to make men virtuous, learned and prosperous. The state is not meant to be man's teacher, pastor and provider all in one—an omnipotent absolute pedagog, to use Rommen's phrase. Nevertheless, it is true to say that a good government is by nature meant to create those social and political conditions conducive to virtue, learning, prosperity—all of which Mill sums up in the phrase: *conduciveness to progress.*

This granted, Mill goes on to say that, ideally, representative government is the best form of government because, better than any other form, it promotes the development of the moral, intellectual and active qualities of the citizen. This it does, because in a representative government, where the people have the last say in how their government should be run, where every citizen has some active share in the affairs of government—a self-reliant, enlightened, well-knit people is thereby developed. People who always have to be on the watch to protect their own rights cannot but grow up active and self-reliant and alive to every danger threatening their liberties. Partaking in government affairs, such as sitting on a jury and the like, is in itself an excellent means of educating the people. Then they learn to "weigh interests not their own; to be guided, in case of conflicting claims, by another rule than their private partialities; to apply at every turn principles and maxims which have for their reason of existence the common good." This fact alone cannot but create a strong bond of national solidarity, "an unselfish identification with the public" —a sentiment which, were it generally lacking in a country, "the utmost aspirations of the lawgiver or the moralist could only stretch to making the bulk of the community a flock of sheep innocently nibbling the grass side by side."

This sorry picture, says Mill, is exactly what obtains under despotism, even in its most benevolent and enlightened form. Under it, despite whatever advantages of prosperity, order and efficiency it may bring, a people is sooner or later reduced to a community of mental dwarfs and slaves. This whole idea he expresses beautifully in the concluding page of his treatise *On Liberty:*

The worth of a state, in the long run, is the worth of individuals composing it; and a state which postpones the interests of their mental expansion and elevation to a little more of administrative skill in the details of business; a state which dwarfs its men in order that they may be more docile instruments in its hands even for beneficial purposes—will find that with small men no great things can really be accomplished; and that the perfection of a machinery to which it has sacrificed everything will in the end avail it nothing, for want of the vital power which, in order that the machine might work more smoothly, it has preferred to banish.

This brief survey hardly does justice to Mill's clever and incisive argumentation in favor of representative government. But one thing is clear: the soundness of Mill's arguments is made possible only because he departs from the orthodox utilitarian doctrines of his youth. He no longer talks like Bentham; he talks more like Coleridge or even Burke. We would have wished, of course, that his advocacy of representative democracy had been based on something more fundamental than the fact that democracy, better than despotism or oligarchy, promotes the mental and moral advancement of a people. We would have wished, for instance, that he had based it on the great medieval principle of immunity from the arbitrary—on the fact that all men are created equal; that because of this essential equality of origin and destiny no man under God has the natural right to dominion: the wise have no right to lord it over the ignorant, nor the strong over the weak, except insofar as they, be they weak or strong, wise or ignorant, have by choice of the people been given the right to command. For in a certain sense it is true to say that democracy, *i.e.,* the rule of the people by the people, is, at the birth of every state, the only legitimate form. *We the people* decide what form of government to choose. Until we have decided that, *we the people* rule.

But from every sign and symptom of our age the unfolding of every modern state into a democratic form seems inevitable: it corresponds to what we might call an intention of nature. Cardinal Manning, a contemporary of Mill, seemed to have already caught this view when he declared: "A new task is before us. The Church has no longer to deal with parliaments and princes, but with the masses and with the people. Whether we will or no, this is our work; we need a new spirit and a new law of life." And not long ago, in his Christmas radio message of 1944, Pope Pius XII cited this view with approval when he said: ". . . in our times, in which the activity of the state is so vast and decisive, the democratic form of government appears to many as a natural demand imposed by reason itself."

We cannot hold back democracy any more than we can hold back the dawn. This seems to be sum and substance of all of Mill's hopes and arguments. Had he remained a thorough and consistent Benthamite to the end, doubtless he would have welcomed without misgivings the inevitable triumph of democracy. As it was, he no longer had the ardent and easy enthusiasms of youth. He still believed that progress and democracy came hand in hand. But the years had brought disillusionments, and disillusionments perspective. What he lost in enthusiasm he gained in wisdom. He now was alive to all the dangers and infirmities of even the best form of government. Chapter VI of his book is a candid unburdening of all his fears. In this he was but echoing Alexis de Tocqueville, whose *Democracy in America* exerted so much influence on Mill and on the writing of *Representative Government*. "The nations of our time," says Tocqueville, "cannot prevent the conditions of man from becoming equal; but it depends upon themselves whether the principle of equality is to lead them to servitude or freedom, to knowledge or barbarism, to prosperity or to wretchedness."

PACIFICO A. ORTIZ

SELECTED BIBLIOGRAPHY

BAIN, Alexander, *John Stuart Mill: A Criticism*. Longmans, Green.

HALÉVY, Élie, *The Growth of Philosophic Radicalism*. London: Faber & Faber.

GRAHAM, William, *English Political Philosophy*. London: Edward Arnold.

M'COSH, James, *An Examination of J. S. Mill's Philosophy*. Scribner.

MILL, John Stuart, *Autobiography*. Columbia University.

MURRAY, Robert H., *English Social and Political Thinkers of the 19th Century*. Cambridge: W. Heffer.

MILL, John Stuart, *Utilitarianism, Liberty, and Representative Government*. Dutton (Everyman's Library).

MILL, John Stuart, *Representative Government* (Chaps. 1-6). Regnery.

Tawney: Religion and the Rise of Capitalism

CAPITALISM IS NOT just an economic system like so many others known from history; it is a system that revolutionized the foundations of the society that bore it, and it still has not spent its revolutionary strength—as is evident in the inroads of capitalism into the Near and Middle East and into the rim of the Far East. In earlier centuries, economic systems changed gradually, without uprooting established forms of religion, ethics, politics and social life. But capitalism, wherever it has spread, has achieved more than a mere change in production and distribution.

Some countries took to capitalism with relative ease; others responded with violent reaction. Examples of the former are England, Holland, the United States; of the latter, Spain, Russia, China. Was it only the influence of economic circumstances that caused the one or the other attitude? There is ample reason to doubt this. There is good reason to believe there are cultural orbits with an affinity to capitalism and others without it. This affinity may wear out, and again it may be acquired slowly. We might perhaps say that present-day Great Britain is losing its historical affinity to capitalism, whereas certain South American countries may be said to be gaining it. However that may be, the historical rise of capitalism took place in countries with a specific affinity to this form of economic life and social structure. What Max Weber and Werner Sombart termed the "spirit of capitalism" was first bred and fostered in England and Holland and found ready acceptance in the United States.

The analysis of capitalism from this viewpoint has been impeded partly by the belief of economic liberals in the natural laws of economic freedom, self-interest and competition; partly by the Marxian thesis of infrastructure and suprastructure, whereby religion, ethics, law and philosophy are held to be the suprastructures—reflexes, as it were, of the truly determining technological factors and of production relations. The dynamics of religion and ethics has thus been obscured or basically denied.

A first breach in this complacent dogmatism was made by Wilhelm Hasbach's study *Philosophical Foundations of the Classical School of Economics,* which was later (1915) to be complemented by the present author's *Inquiries into Classical Economics.* Meanwhile, however, Max Weber's articles on "Protestant Ethic and the Spirit of Capitalism" had traced one of the roots of the capitalist spirit to Calvinism, in particular to the British nonconformist (Puritan) branch of Calvinism. His emphasis rested on the "calling": the individual is called to labor for God in two spheres, the spiritual and the temporal. His success in the temporal sphere may indicate that he belongs to the "elect." Hence the release of tremendous energies in things temporal—and they run amok when the subordination of temporal to spiritual ceases—that is, when secularism dries up the religious source.

Weber's thesis gave rise to an ever-increasing flood of literature on the problem of the relationship between religion and ethics, on the one hand, and economic life on the other. We mention only some of the outstanding names: Lujo Brentano, who contested (as did Felix Rachfahl) the thesis as presented by Weber, whereas Ernst Troeltsch sided with Weber and enlarged the analysis in his *Social Teaching of the Christian Churches.* Werner Sombart felt inclined to ascribe the rise of the capitalist spirit to the Jews. H. G. Wood, William Ashley and William Cunningham made substantial clarifications of the issue, as did Christopher Dawson. Liberals and medievalists alike thought to have a stake in the issue, the ones glorying, the others indicating. Uhlhorn, a well-known German protagonist of the superiority of Protestantism over Catholicism, had already in the nineties declared that the machine had "something Protestant" about it and that Catholic countries were economically and socially backward solely because they were Catholic. The present author well remembers a schoolteacher remarking to her class, "This country [Spain] is Catholic, therefore backward."

Such was the state of affairs when the Holland Memorial Lectures invited the brilliant English historian R. H. Tawney to deliver the first lectures at King's College, London, in 1922. The deed of foundation of the Holland Memorial Lectures stipulates that the subject of the triennial lectures shall be "The Religion of the Incarnation in Its Bearing on the Social and Economic Life of Man." Tawney enlarged his lectures into the book here under discussion. His study has become a classic in the field.

The central theme of the book is the influence of religion and ethics on the formation of the political, economic and social ideas during the crucial centuries of the Western world, the sixteenth and seventeenth. Tawney is far from stating a merely spiritual interpretation of this phase of history: he places due stress on economic and socio-economic factors. He makes it clear, for example, that the medieval background exercised its influence far beyond the sixteenth century among High Church men and nonconformists alike, and certainly on Lutheranism. According to him, it was exactly the tremendous change in economic and social circumstances which rendered the traditional economic ethics obsolete.

Again, the transition from medieval social ethics to Puritan business ethics was likewise due to changes in economic environment and conditions. He says, parenthetically, "The traditional teachings were abandoned because, on the whole, they deserved to be abandoned" (p. 185) as the social doctrines advanced from the pulpits "offered . . . little guidance. Their practical ineffectiveness prepared the way for their theoretical abandonment." Obviously it was not only the economic change but also the lack of guidance (in this particular case by the Church of England) which led to abandoning the traditional ethics. Had the Church "not ceased to think," her social teaching would not have ceased to count (p. 185).

Tawney is convinced that the revolution in the ethics and economic life of that period was not directly due to the Reformation—usury was not "the brat of heresy," as a seventeenth-century pamphleteer would have it. "The revolt from Rome," says Tawney, "synchronized, both in Germany and England, with a period of acute social distress." He finds it cannot be said that there existed a "logical connection between changes in economic organization and changes in religious doctrine" (p. 83). Economic individualism frequently is charged to religious innovations— either as an opprobrium or as a eulogy.

Tawney differs: "If it is true that the Reformation released forces which were to act as a solvent of the traditional attitude of religious thought to social and economic issues, it did so without design, and against the intention of most reformers. In reality, however sensational the innovations in economic practice which accompanied the expansion of financial capitalism in the sixteenth century, the development of doctrine on the subject of economic ethics was continuous, and the more closely it is examined, the less foundation does there seem to be for the view that the stream plunged into vacancy over the precipice of religious revolution. To think of the abdication of religion from its theoretical primacy over economic activity and social institutions as synchronizing with the revolt from Rome, is to antedate a movement which was not finally accomplished for another century and a half, and which owed as much to changes in economic and political organization as it did to developments in the sphere of religious thought" (p. 85).

To be sure, "princes and nobles and businessmen conducted themselves after their kind, and fished eagerly in troubled waters, but the aim of religious leaders was to reconstruct not merely doctrine and ecclesiastical government, but conduct and institutions, on a pattern derived from the forgotten purity of primitive Christianity" (85). The ethical doctrine of the medieval Church was adopted by the reformers; in the case of Luther, Tawney finds even a falling back behind the late medieval ethics as represented by St. Antonine of Florence: "Compared with the lucid and subtle rationalism of a thinker like St. Antonine, his [Luther's] sermons and pamphlets on social questions make an impression of naïveté, as of an impetuous but ill-informed genius, dispensing with the cumbrous embarrassments of law and logic" (p. 88).

Tawney does not find any validity in the claim that capitalism was the product of the Reformation, or that it is a specific phenomenon of the eighteenth and nineteenth centuries. According to him, capitalism had existed "on a grand scale" both in medieval Italy and in medieval Flanders; and capitalist "temper" ("which is prepared to sacrifice all moral scruples to the pursuit of profit") had been all too familiar to the saints and sages of the Middle Ages. Capitalism and a wage earner's stratum characterized Florence and Venice in the period of their glory; and the urge for gain and greed ran through the whole Middle Ages—as much as did the struggle against usury and injustice. Avarice and greed in high places had prevailed. However, "it is something to have insisted that the law of charity is binding," and "it is not less important to observe that men called these vices by their right names, and had not learned to persuade themselves that greed was enterprise and avarice economy" (p. 60).

Right here Tawney discovers the great divide between pre-capitalistic and capitalistic eras. Something decisive happened with the advent of Puritanism, and it took a century and a half for it to reach its full significance. The decisive thing which happened was the identification of private business interest with the common good, and secularized Puritanism offered this identification. The tremendous storm of the "soldier-saints," "humble to God, haughty to man," ended in the utilitarian weakness that religious liberty was a considerable advantage, "regarded merely in a commercial view" (Josiah Tucker, *A Brief Essay*, 1750). In the sweep of his identification, the Church of England relaxed and finally gave up all social controls. Whereas, the law of nature was invoked by medieval writers as a moral restraint upon economic self-interest, by the seventeenth century nature had come "to connote not divine ordinance but human appetites, and natural rights were invoked by the individualism of the age as the reason why self-interests should be given free play" (p. 180).

The phases of development may be summed up in the following way: early Puritanism preserved the medieval ethical notions and tried to observe them more strictly in practice. Economic conditions and social structure, however, changed tremendously during exactly those decades. In the ensuing tension and conflict, business ethics finally got the upper hand—the secularization of Puritanism was one decisive fact in the formation of the capitalistic spirit and, consequently, in the new world this spirit created.

We cannot go into the details of the brilliant chapter "Medieval Background," or of the chapters on Lutheranism, the Church of England and Calvinism. Suffice it to say that Tawney ascribes the spiritual dynamism behind the rise of the modern capitalistic spirit to that one and radical branch among Calvinist denominations, Puritanism. Like Calvinism, it had begun "by being the very soul of authoritarian regimentation. It ended by being the vehicle of an almost utilitarian individualism." In its beginning it set all human interests and activities within the compass of religion and tried to formulate a Christian casuistry of economic conduct; but the Puritans succeeded "even less than the Popes and the Doctors whose teaching, not always unwittingly, they repeated, and their failure had its roots not merely in the obstacles offered by the ever more recalcitrant opposition of a commercial environment, but, like all failures which are significant, in the soul of Puritanism itself" (226).

The Puritan sought God in isolation from his fellow men; his moral self-sufficiency nerved his will but corroded his sense of social solidarity. "For, if each individual's destiny hangs on a private transaction between himself and his Maker, what room is left for social intervention? . . . A spiritual aristocrat, who sacrificed fraternity to liberty, he drew from his idealization of personal responsibility a theory of individual rights, which, secularized and generalized, was to be among the most potent explosives that the world has known. He drew from it also a scale of social values in which the traditional scheme of Christian virtues was almost exactly reversed, and which, since he was above all things practical, he carried as a dynamic into the routine of business and political life" (p. 230).

As early as 1709 a Scottish divine might have remarked that "the Lord was frowning upon our trade . . . since it was put in the room of religion"; he had not grasped what slowly became the reality: that to the Puritan mind "money-making, if not free from spiritual dangers, could be and ought to be carried on for the greater glory of God"—and as proof that one was a member of the Chosen Few. The temporal "calling," originally only the handmaid of the spiritual calling, finally won out.

To the Puritan it appeared as a "fortunate dispensation" that virtues enjoined on Christians—diligence, moderation, sobriety, thrift—were the very qualities most conducive to commercial success (p. 245). The "lean Goddess, Abstinence, which Mr. Keynes, in a passage of brilliant indiscretion, has revealed as the tutelary divinity of Victorian England, was inducted to the austere splendours of her ascetic shrine by the pious hands of Puritan moralists" (p. 251). To a generation of later Puritans a "creed which transformed the acquisition of wealth from a drudgery or a temptation into a moral duty was the milk of lions. It was not that religion was expelled from practical life but that religion itself gave it a foundation of granite. . . . The good Christian was not wholly dissimilar from the economic man" (p. 253).

Economic ambitions and the efficiency drive are good servants if harnessed to a social purpose; they turn the mill and grind the corn. But they are bad masters. "Economic efficiency is a necessary element in the life of any sane and vigorous society. . . . But to convert efficiency from an instrument into a primary object is to destroy efficiency itself." Effective action in a complex civilization demands cooperation; and cooperation demands agreement as to the ends of the effort and the criteria by which success is judged. Agreement as to ends requires a standard of values; and this standard cannot itself be merely economic; there must be some conception of the requirements of human nature as a whole, "since even quite common men have souls." Therefore: "no increase in material wealth will compensate them for arrangements which insult their self-respect and impair their freedom" (p. 284).

Our short presentation in no way conveys a picture of the depth and brilliance of Tawney's book. To a generation of scholars prone to call for and indulge in so-called "facts," while ignorant of the significance of ethics and spiritual values, he presents both the facts and their spiritual background. He, like Max Weber, belongs to the pioneers in a field strangely neglected by the vast stream of historical and social research on the origins of capitalism, namely, in the field of the metaeconomic and metapolitical conditions of capitalism. He, like Weber, believes that something decisive happened in the sixteenth and seventeenth centuries. He, like Weber, found that the "logic" of the Reformation (rather than its attachment to the social ethics of the past) "riveted on the social thought of Protestantism a dualism which, as its implications were developed, emptied religion of its social content, and society of its soul" (p. 101).

However, Tawney visualizes capitalism as a potential menace to every civilization. According to him, greed and covetousness may break through religious and ethical codes in any historical phase, provided economic and social circumstances are propitious. In proof thereof he cites Florence and Flanders of pre-Reformation fame and claims for them the character of fully developed capitalist economies. Now, in the first place it seems to me that capitalism cannot be reduced to greed and covetousness, to avarice and lust for economic power; these vices are functionally and structurally "multivalent"; they need not produce the functional and structural system of modern capitalism. Furthermore, we grant that there existed capitalistic enterprises long before the rise of capitalism—however, capitalistic enterprises are not yet capitalism, any more than the small stratum of *mercenarii* of the thirteenth century were a proletariat. It would follow that Weber was more correct when he identified capitalism as a unique occidental phenomenon.

Again, on the other hand, Tawney is perfectly correct in stressing the role of external factors in the rise of capitalism: economic developments, discoveries, etc., and the role of internal factors other than religion and ethics: intellectual movements deriving from the Renaissance. I think Tawney is correct, too, in his statement that Weber oversimplified Calvinism itself: the social ethics of sixteenth-century Geneva did differ from the ethics of seventeenth-century Puritans, and seventeenth-century Puritanism was far from presenting one doctrine with regard to business ethics. And yet, when all is said and done, Tawney goes a long way with Max Weber's fundamental thesis.

One more word in concluding: the book here reviewed brings home the truth that the secularization of originally religious and ethical doctrines is a dynamic factor of first rank in the history of Western civilization. Who will write us the Great Book on "The Rise and Fall of Western Civilization Under the Impact of Secularism"?

GOETZ A. BRIEFS

SELECTED BIBLIOGRAPHY

FANFANI, A., *Protestantism, Catholicism and Capitalism*. Sheed & Ward.
WEBER, MAX, *The Protestant Ethic and the Spirit of Capitalism*. London: Allen & Unwin.
VON SCHULZE-GAEVERNITZ, *Democracy and Religion*. London: Allen & Unwin.
DAWSON, C., *Religion and Progress*. Sheed & Ward.
TAWNEY, R. H., *Religion and the Rise of Capitalism*. Mentor (New American Library).

Notes on the Contributors

REV. RUDOLPH ARBESMANN, O.S.A. [1895-   ]

After early education in his natal Fürth, Germany, Father Arbesmann attended the universities of Würzburg, Munich and Rome. He was ordained in Rome in 1923 and received his doctorate at the University of Würzburg in 1929. That same year he sat for the state examination in classics, history and Germanic languages at the same university. He was assistant professor of classics at the Humanistisches Gymnasium, Münnesstadt, Bavaria (1930-1931) and at the International College St. Monica, Rome (1931-1934), and professor of ancient history and archeology at the Universidad Católica, Santiago, Chile (1934-1937). Coming to the United States, he was appointed assistant professor of classics at Fordham in 1937 and has been associate professor since 1944. He is the author of three volumes in German on classical subjects, and in addition to contributing to German encyclopedias, also writes frequently for such journals as the *Classical Weekly, Classical Bulletin, Traditio, Thought, The Americas*. He is a coeditor of the series on The Fathers of the Church published by the Newman Bookshop.

GOETZ A. BRIEFS [1889-   ]

Labor economics is Dr. Briefs's field, for which he was prepared by studies at the universities of Bonn, Munich and Freiburg. He was a lecturer at the last-named university from 1913 to 1921; associate professor at the University of Würzburg in 1922; professor of economics at the University of Freiburg (1923-1926) and at the University of Berlin (1926-1934). On coming to the United States, Dr. Briefs was visiting professor at the Catholic University of America (1934-1937), and has been professor of labor economics at Georgetown University (Graduate School) since 1937. He has published in this country *The Proletariat: a Challenge to Western Civilization,* and in German a study pertinent to the issue of Mr. Tawney's book: *Inquiry into Classical Economics.* He contributes as well to a large number of publications in the fields of labor, cartels, industrial relations and the like.

FRANCIS X. CONNOLLY [1909- *now dead*]

Having received his bachelor's and master's degrees from Fordham University (1930 and 1933), Dr. Connolly won his Ph.D. from the same institution in 1937. He is at present Associate Professor of English at the University and Chairman of the College English Department. He has edited two anthologies of verse, is coeditor of *Return to Poetry,* author of *Literature, the Channel of Culture* and coeditor of *Stories of Our Century.* He has contributed articles and reviews to many periodicals, including *America, Commonweal, The Catholic World, Spirit* and *Thought.* He is one of the editors of the Catholic Book Club, and has been an editor of *Spirit* since its foundation in 1933. He served as Chairman of the Board of Directors of the Catholic Poetry Society for eight years. During World War II he was a lieutenant in the United States Navy. He is a member of the board of directors and past president of the New York Conference of College Teachers of English.

REV. CHARLES DENECKE, S.J. [1907-   ]

Father Denecke's A.B. and M.A. degrees are from Woodstock College, Woodstock, Md. Georgetown University granted him the degree of Ph.D. in 1945 in philosophy. Father Denecke taught literature and the classics at St. Joseph's College, Philadelphia, from 1931 to 1934, and in 1942 was appointed Professor of Philosophy at the University of Scranton. In 1946 he was recalled to Woodstock College as Professor of Philosophy, which position he still holds. He has been a frequent contributor of book reviews to *Best Sellers* (Scranton).

REV. HAROLD C. GARDINER, S.J. [1902-   ]

A native of Washington, D. C., Father Gardiner entered the Society of Jesus in 1922. After classical studies at St. Andrew-on-Hudson, Poughkeepsie, N. Y., philosophical studies at Woodstock College, Woodstock, Md., a period of teaching the classics and English at Canisius College, Buffalo, N. Y., he returned to Woodstock for theological studies and ordination. A year of ascetical theology in Belgium was succeeded by his entering Downing College, Cambridge University, for postgraduate work in English. The outbreak of the war forced his return to the United States in 1940, but he was able to receive his Ph.D. from Cambridge *in absentia* in 1941. Since 1940 he has been Literary Editor of *America*. He is also Editorial Chairman of the Catholic Book Club and of the Catholic Children's Book Club. His published work, in addition to articles and reviews in *America* and other periodicals, includes *Mysteries End*, a study of the cessation of the medieval religious stage (Yale University Press, 1945), *Tenets for Readers and Reviewers* (America Press, 1942, 1947). The series of articles on the Great Books comprising this volume are a continuation of a series which appeared originally under his editorship in *America*.

WALDEMAR GURIAN [1902-   ]

now dead

Born in St. Petersburg, Russia, Dr. Gurian pursued his earlier studies at the universities of Bonn, Breslau and Munich. He received his doctorate from the University of Cologne in 1923. He came to the United States in 1927 and has become a citizen. Since 1937 he has been professor of political science at Notre Dame University, and since 1938 Editor of *The Review of Politics*. His published books include *Bolshevism, The Rise and Decline of Marxism, Hitler and the Christians*, and *French Nationalism*. He contributes articles to *Foreign Affairs, Dublin Review, American Historical Review, American Political Science Review, America, The Commonweal* and others.

VICTOR M. HAMM [1904-   ]

Educated by the Jesuits in both high school and college (Marquette), Dr. Hamm did his graduate work at Harvard, receiving his M.A. in 1929 and his Ph.D. in 1932. He was Sheldon Traveling Fellow from Harvard in 1932-1933, studying in England, France and Italy. He has taught English at St. Louis University and at the College of Mt. St. Joseph-on-the-Ohio. Since 1937 he has been Professor of English at Marquette University. His articles have appeared in *America, Thought, Modern Language Notes, PMLA* and *Philological Quarterly*. Essays by his hand have been included in *Irving Babbitt as Man and Teacher* and in *Jesuit Thinkers of the Renaissance*. He is the translator of *The March to Liberation* by Yves Simon, and his *Pico della Mirandola: of Unity and Being* was published by Marquette University Press in 1943.

RILEY HUGHES [1914-   ]

Riley Hughes, a graduate of Providence College, did his graduate work in English at Yale and Brown universities and in philosophy at Georgetown University. He was assistant in English at Brown University in 1938-1939. From 1940 to 1942 he was state editor and supervisor of the Connecticut Writers' Project. From 1942 to 1946 he was Assistant professor of English and Director of Public Relations at Providence College. Since 1946 he has been Lecturer in English at the School of Foreign Service, Georgetown University. He is the author of *Our Coast Guard Academy* (1944) and a regular contributor of literary articles and reviews to *America, The Commonweal, Renascence, The Saturday Review of Literature, The Thomist* and *Thought*.

LOUIS J. A. MERCIER [1880-   ]

Dr. Mercier is an emeritus of Harvard University, where for thirty-five years he taught courses in French literature and in education. He is now Professor of Comparative Philosophy and Literature at Georgetown University and Visiting Professor (summers) at l'Université de Montréal and l'Université Laval at Quebec. His degrees include Litt.D., L.H.D., D.Sc., Ed., Dr. es Lettres, LL.D. His publications include many articles in Catholic and non-Catholic reviews and professional journals in the United States, Canada and France. He is the author of four French textbooks, of *Our Lady of the Birds,* and of three books on humanism: *Le Mouvement Humaniste aux États-Unis,* crowned by the French Academy, *The Challenge of Humanism* and *American Humanism and the New Age*. Dr. Mercier appeared in Volume I of *The Great Books* with a study of Rousseau's *The Social Contract*.

JEAN PAUL MISRAHI [1910-   ]

Columbia University granted Dr. Misrahi his A.B. in 1929 and his doctorate in 1933. He has studied at the universities of Paris and Nancy. He was an instructor in romance languages at Brooklyn College from 1933 to 1938. Since 1938 he has been Professor, Associate Professor and Head of the Department of Romance Languages at Fordham University Graduate School.

He is a contributor to *Liturgical Arts, Speculum, The French Review* and other magazines. He is a member of the editorial board of *Thought* and the author of *Le Roman des Sept Sages.* Dr. Misrahi contributed a study of *The Essays of Montaigne* to Volume I of *The Great Books.*

Rev. Pacifico A. Ortiz, S.J. [1913-   ]

Father Ortiz made his classical, philosophical and theological studies at the Jesuit Seminary in Manila, Philippines, and received his S.T.L. from Woodstock College, Maryland. Before the war he taught philosophy at the Ateneo de Manila, Philippines. During the war he served as chaplain on Corregidor and later as personal chaplain to the late President Quezon of the Philippines. He is at present working for his Ph.D. degree in political philosophy at Fordham University.

Rev. Edwin A. Quain, S.J. [1906-   ]

Father Quain's college degrees of A.B. and M.A. were obtained at Woodstock College, Maryland. His S.T.L. is from the same institution, in 1937. His doctorate in the classics was granted by Harvard University in 1941. From 1941 to 1945 he was an instructor in the classics in the Fordham University Graduate School; since 1945 he has been an assistant professor in the same subject. He is Editor of the Fordham University Studies and a contributor to *America, Traditio,* the *Classical Bulletin, Thought* and *Speculum.* He is a collaborator in "The Fathers of the Church in Translation." He is author of "St. Jerome and Humanism" in *A Monument to St. Jerome* (Sheed & Ward, 1948) and of "The Medieval Accessus ad Auctores," *Traditio III,* 215-264. Father Quain appeared in Volume I of *The Great Books* with an essay, Aristophanes: *Lysistrata, Birds, Clouds.*

Balduin Victor Schwarz [1902-   ]

Dr. Schwarz's graduate studies were made at the universities of Heidelberg, Cologne and Munich. He received his doctor's degree from the last-named institution. He was for some time an Assistant Professor in the Graduate School at the University of Muenster. He left Germany voluntarily in 1933 on the rise of Hitler and taught at various universities and colleges in Switzerland, Austria and France. At the fall of France, he was invited to come to this country on a Rockefeller Foundation fellowship. He is at present Professor of Philosophy at Seton Hill College, Greensburg, Pennsylvania. In addition to contributing frequent articles to scientific journals, he is the author of three books in German: *Psychology of Tears, Error as a Philosophical Problem* and *Perennial Philosophy.* In the first volume of *The Great Books* he contributed the article, Aristotle: *Politics, Book I.*

Dietrich von Hildebrand [1889-   ]

Earlier studies in Munich and Goettingen were crowned by Dr. von Hildebrand by his doctorate degree (Goettingen) in 1912. He taught at the University of Munich from 1919 to 1933. Hitler's rise to power forced him to Vienna, where he was a Professor at the university until 1938. He was founder and editor of the Catholic anti-Nazi magazine *Der Christliche*

Ständestaat. Repudiating Nazism once again, he went to Toulouse as professor at the Catholic University, 1939-1940, and finally came to the United States. He has been Professor of Philosophy at Fordham University since 1941 and has become an American citizen. In addition to many works in German, he is author of *In Defense of Purity, Liturgy and Personality* and *Transformation in Christ.* To Volume I of *The Great Books* he contributed the study of Aristotle's *Ethics, Book I.*

REV. GUSTAVE WEIGEL, S.J. [1906-196_]

Father Weigel's A.B. and M.A. are from Woodstock College, Woodstock, Md. Following his ordination in 1934, he went to Rome for graduate ecclesiastical studies. He received the degree of S.T.D. from the Gregorian University in 1938. For eleven years following he was prominent in the academic life of Chile, where he was professor of philosophy and theology and Dean of the School of Divinity of the Catholic University of Chile. Since 1948 he has been professor of Ecclesiology at Woodstock College. He has written several works in Spanish and was the founder of the *Anales de la Facultad de Teología,* an annual review of theology.